A Tailgater's Guide
to
LSU Football

Dedicated to

∽ **Philip F. Warner** ∽

September 19, 1947 - May 21, 2007

Avid Tiger tailgater, father, friend

Foreword

The pageantry of tailgating outside Tiger Stadium goes beyond the incredible food and consumption of beverages. The passion and love of LSU Football truly runs through the veins of all Tiger faithful. Hospitality is at full force when opposing fans visit nearby parties only to find Tiger fans anxiously waiting to nourish their rivals with Cajun cuisine and libations. The greatest feeling in the world occurs about an hour before kickoff. While watching the energy level outside the stadium increase by the second, you can't help think, "There's no place I'd rather be than Tiger Stadium on a Saturday Night!"

– Ruffin Rodrigue, 2007

* Ruffin Rodrigue is a former All-SEC LSU offensive lineman who played from 1986 to 1989. Today he is a restaurateur in Baton Rouge, serving as part-owner and manager of Ruffino's Italian Restaurant off I-10.

Preface

Since I wrote the original *Tailgater's Guide To SEC Football* in 2000, I have come in contact with thousands of fans from across the Southeastern Conference. The nation's most powerful league has some of the most impressive fans! While the conference book format is ideal for the avid SEC tailgater, it falls short of a more comprehensive review of each school's unique history and traditions. This new book, *A Tailgater's Guide To LSU Football*, is a special look into what makes the LSU Football game day experience like no other! Inside learn about LSU's fascinating and colorful history on the gridiron; it's greatest coaches, teams and players; and even tailgating recipes for those of you who like to put your money where your mouth is. Bon Appetit, Tiger fans!

– Chris Warner, 2007

Introduction

Tailgating is logically fun. It's a pairing of the Deep South's most treasured values and traditions. On selected Saturdays each autumn, family and football combine. Friends share food against a nostalgic university backdrop. It's a moment in time sought by hundreds of thousands of alumni and fans. Today, the practiced art of tailgating has become enormously popular. LSU fans, however, may have cornered the market on the burgeoning cultural practice. Tiger game days showcase virtual tailgating tent cities in a confluence of crowded purple and gold canopies. Use this definitive guide to LSU Football to educate your extended tailgating family on the unique history and traditions of the LSU Football Program. Charles McClendon once said of LSU's great tradition, "Some programs have forgotten their tradition. LSU's tradition is great. I hope LSU never forgets its tradition."

Table of Contents

1 The Southeastern Conference

In February of 1933, Dr. Frank L. McVey, President of the University of Kentucky, and one of the South's leading educators, was elected the first president of the Southeastern Conference. Thirteen members of the SEC's predecessor, the Southern Conference, all became charter members of the new conference. They were: Alabama, Alabama Polytechnic Institute (now Auburn University), University of Florida, Georgia Institute of Technology, University of Georgia, University of Kentucky, Louisiana State University, Mississippi State University, University of Mississippi, University of the South, University of Tennessee, Tulane University, and Vanderbilt University.

Tulane University, Georgia Tech and the University of the South eventually vacated the SEC, leaving only the ten founding member schools. Tulane, a charter member, left the league at the end of the

1965-66 academic year. The Green Wave football team competed as an independent from 1966 until 1996, and eventually joined Conference USA. Georgia Tech later joined the Metro Conference in 1975 for all sports except football for three years from 1975-1978. Today Tech is a member of the Atlantic Coast Conference.

The modern SEC comprises twelve schools representing ten separate Southern states. Six member institutions—Alabama, Arkansas, Auburn, LSU, Ole Miss, and Mississippi State make up the Western Division of the conference. Another six schools form the Eastern Division—Florida, Georgia, Kentucky, South Carolina, Tennessee and Vanderbilt.

The Southeastern Conference received a facelift in 1990 when Arkansas and South Carolina were added to the mix. This landmark addition boosted the enrollment to twelve schools, six within each separate directional division. Furthermore, a championship game pitting the top two teams from each division was implemented in 1992 in order to decide, on the playing field, a true conference champion for the first time during the league's history. Since these changes, the "new and improved" SEC has outperformed college football's preeminent conferences.

Since the expansion of the Southeastern Conference and the beginning of the practice of playing a championship game in 1992, the SEC has five times won the national championship—Alabama in 1992, Florida in 1996, Tennessee in 1998, LSU in 2003 and Florida in 2006. Since 1992 the SEC and the Big 12 have won more national championships than any other conference. The SEC has won 4 titles with three different schools while the Big 12 has equaled the mark with two different schools.

Since the first season of the Bowl Championship Series in 1998, the SEC leads all conferences with three national championships. Tennessee won the BCS' first national title in 1998, LSU won the crown in 2003 and Florida defeated Ohio State in 2007. The Big 12 has won two while the ACC, Big Ten Pac-10 and Big East have won BCS titles.

SEC Record Last Five+ Seasons (2002-06)

	W-L	Pct.	Bowls	SEC Champ	AP Top 25
Georgia	53-13	.803	5	2	5
*LSU	52-13	.800	5	1	4
Auburn	50-14	.781	6	1	4
Florida	45-19	.703	5	1	3
Tennessee	42-21	.667	4	0	3
Arkansas	37-26	.587	3	0	1
Alabama	36-27	.571	3	0	2
South Carolina	31-29	.517	2	0	0
Ole Miss	28-32	.467	2	0	1
Kentucky	24-35	.407	1	0	0
Vanderbilt	15-43	.259	0	0	0
Miss. State	14-44	.241	0	0	0

* *Over the last five seasons LSU has the second-best winning percentage of the 12 SEC schools.*

Louisiana State University is a member of the nation's most powerful athletic conference, the storied and tradition-rich, Southeastern. The twelve-member institution SEC is the paragon of the college athletic experience. During its storied, 74 year existence the Southeastern Conference has evolved into the most impressive league of organized, intercollegiate gridiron competition in the history of the United States.

No other Division I football-playing conference can boast of the many accolades and attendance records that the SEC currently holds. Furthermore, the SEC has appeared in (352) and won (177) more bowl games and has produced more All-American football players than any other conference. Moreover, since 2000, the SEC has more bowl appearances (52) and bowl bowl wins (29) than any other conference.

2

Louisiana State University (LSU)

Pronounced: "Ellesshoe."

LOUISIANA IS A POLITICALLY EXOTIC, ethnically and culturally diverse state that rallies indomitably around its favorite college football team—the Bayou Bengal Tigers of Baton Rouge. The old adage goes that there's only one thing more exciting than Louisiana politics . . . and that's Tiger football on Saturday night in Death Valley, LSU's storied sunken football stadium built by former demagogue Governor Huey Pierce Long. With a capacity for 92,600 rabid, Mediterranean-blooded fans, on selected autumn sabbaths vaunted Tiger Stadium becomes more populous than many of Louisiana's larger cities. The mantra of the fun-loving Cajuns from South Louisiana is "Laissez les bons temps roulez!" or "Let the good times roll!" Weekend festivals are a common thread within the state's cultural fabric. It is no wonder every LSU fan across the Bayou State anxiously awaits home football games. That's because every LSU Football game is not only a chance for fans to see their venerable Tigers play—it's also a huge tailgating party complete with all the trappings of a bona fide Louisiana festival—good food, friends and fun! Louisiana's Flagship University, Louisiana State University in Baton Rouge is both a land and sea grant institution, one of only a handful of universities in America to hold such a distinction.

Memorial Bell Tower

LSU. In 1853 the Louisiana General Assembly established the Louisiana State Seminary of Learning and Military Academy near Pineville. The university opened January 2, 1860, with Colonel William Tecumseh Sherman as superintendent. The school closed in 1863 due to the Civil War. The Seminary reopened its doors in October of 1865, only to be burned in October of 1869, four years later. In November of 1869 the school resumed its exercises in Baton Rouge, where it has remained. Land for the current campus was acquired in 1918, and construction started in 1922. Formal dedication of the present campus occurred on April 30, 1926.

LSU's strong military heritage earned it the nickname "Ole War Skule." The moniker was formerly a popular reference to LSU at the turn of the twentieth century, as was the term "Old Lou." Three LSU presidents were generals in the armed forces. Until 1969, ROTC was mandatory for all entering freshmen and during that time LSU produced as many officers for World War II as West Point, Annapolis or Texas A&M.

William Tecumseh Sherman, who served as a general for the Union Army during the Civil War, was LSU's first superintendent. Sherman was superintendent prior to the start of the bloody conflict that in some extreme cases, pitted Southern brothers and cousins fighting against one another. After great duress, Sherman sided with the United States Constitution. However, his fondness for the "Ole War Skule" softened somewhat his hard-line stance toward the Confederacy. Remarkably, at Sherman's request, his troops sacked and burned wholesale portions of the rest of the Deep South; but the Louisiana State Seminary, as well as other Louisiana homes and cities, were spared. Many of these beautiful antebellum antiquities survive today.

LSU *is* Baton Rouge. The state's flagship calls Baton Rouge its home and its sports teams—especially Tiger football—inspire unparalleled loyalty among its rabid fan base. Louisiana's capital city is the heart of plantation country in the Deep South. The city contains the largest concentration of plantation homes along the Mississippi River corridor. And the name—Baton Rouge? It means "Red Stick," and it refers to the ancient Indian custom of using a red stick, or baton to mark the boundary between two Indian tribes.

Baton Rouge is also a great venue for popular rock bands, such as the area's own homegrown Better Than Ezra, which got its meteoric start in Red Stick in the late 1980's. One Ezra song, titled *This Time of Year*, was written on the way to an LSU-Ole Miss game in Oxford.

3   LSU by the Numbers

Enrollment: 33,000
Alumni: 170,000
Faculty & Staff: 5,000
Countries represented by students: 125
Majors: 73 separate fields of study
Founded: 1860 (Pineville, Louisiana)
Baton Rouge campus founded: 1926
Years playing football: 113 (1893)
Number of national championships: 43
LSU's libraries contain over 3.2 million volumes
LSU Campus information: (225) 578-3202

4   LSU Football

FOOTBALL AT LSU began in 1893 under the direction of Dr. Charles E. Coates, a chemistry professor from Baltimore, Maryland. When Coates arrived in Baton Rouge in the early 1890's he was surprised that football had not yet been established. That fall he issued a request for football players. He later remarked that "some mighty good-looking prospects" reported. Coates was assisted that first year by Harcourt A. Morgan, a young professor of entomology and zoology who had learned Canadian rugby prior to coming to LSU and who later became President of the University of Tennessee. Dr. Coates was so determined to outfit his fledgling team that he reportedly drove nails into his players' shoes in order for them to have cleats. That year the Tigers posted an 0-1 record, losing to Tulane in New Orleans. By 1896 the schedule had increased to six games, with LSU winning all of them.

Azaleas at Charles Coates

The advent of electric lamps allowed for the first night game in Tiger Stadium to be played in 1931. Night football allowed for cooler game time temperatures and resulted in increased attendance. Moreover, it allowed the rudiments of tailgating to become a day-long, anticipated, festive event that continues to this day. Night ball games continued unabated until the early 1970's when televised day games forced fans to flock to the campus, thereby abandoning their prior practice of party-hopping from house-to-house. Legend has it that the Tigers play better at night. However, statistics prove it. From 1960-2006 LSU won nearly 80 percent of its night games in Death Valley. Moreover, Louisiana State University was the first Southeastern Conference school to have a squad of female dancers accompany their football team and perform at halftime. The glamorous "Golden Girls" were copied almost overnight by the other competing SEC schools.

5 Nickname

DRAWN FROM THE LEGENDARY Confederate battalion—Robert E. Lee's "Louisiana Tigers," who distinguished themselves during the Shenandoah Valley Campaign in Virginia under Major Chatham Roberdeau Wheat. The 1st Louisiana Special Battalion, or Wheat's Tigers Company "B" as it was known, was an elite fighting regiment consisting of New Orleans "Zouaves" and Donaldsonville "Cannonneers" that was so renowned for their battle ferocity and rough and readiness that fellow Confederate troops were reluctant to fight alongside the licentious lot. The notorious Pelican State warriors earned their nickname from an uncompromising and unflinching battle style. Their intrepid sacrifices forged a proud legacy that lives today, personified by the LSU Tiger spirit. During the fall of 1896, LSU Football Coach A.W. Jeardeau's squad posted a perfect 6-0 record, and it was in that fourth gridiron campaign that LSU adopted the Tiger moniker for its team.

6   Colors

ROYAL PURPLE AND GOLD. The inception of LSU's colors is linked to the Louisiana carnival known as Mardi Gras, which means "Fat Tuesday" in French. In November 1893, LSU played its first football game against Tulane University. Upon arrival to the Crescent City, LSU's head coach, Charles Coates, realized that his team's gray uniforms were drab in comparison to Tulane's olive green outfits. This prompted the LSU coach to purchase purple and gold ribbons at a nearby store to adorn the Tiger uniforms. Because of Mardi Gras, the store (Reymond's at the corner of Third and Main Streets) had plenty of purple and gold material (Traditional Carnival colors are purple, gold and green). Team Captain E.B. Young reportedly hand-picked the colors for the Tigers. LSU's first academic colors were blue and white.

7   Mascot

NAMED AFTER THE ORIGINAL Tiger trainer, Mike Chambers, "Mike the Tiger," a live Bengal Tiger, is LSU's revered mascot. Tradition dictates that for every growl by Mike before a football game, the Tigers will score a touchdown that night. Mike rides through Tiger Stadium in his cage on wheels before every football game and is cared for by the students at the LSU Vet School. Mike I was purchased with student contributions in 1936 from the Little Rock Zoo. Mike V, LSU's last mascot, died in 2007. Mike's ride through Tiger Stadium before home games in a cage topped by LSU cheerleaders is a school tradition. Before entering the stadium, his wheeled cage is parked next to the opponent's locker room in the stadium's southeast end. Opposing players must make their way past Mike's cage to reach their locker room.

Mike the Tiger

8   Facilities

AS COMPETITIVE AS modern head football coaches are in terms of recruiting top athletes, programs today are equally competitive in terms of facility development, maintenance and expansion. Most if not all of the Southeastern Conference schools have recently engaged in an aggressive expansion of their athletic facilities for both the athlete and fan. LSU is no exception to this noticeable trend. In 2001 Tiger Stadium expanded to a capacity of 92,600 with the addition of dozens of state-of-the art luxury boxes. Additionally, the $14 million Cox Communications Academic Center for Athletes was unveiled inside the old Huey P. Long Fieldhouse in an effort to enhance the importance of academics for LSU's student athlete. Furthermore, the $15 million Football Operations Center replete with four outdoor fields, an indoor practice facility, locker room, training room, video operations center and equipment room near the current LSU practice field were completed in 2005.

Charles McClendon Practice Facility:

The Charles McClendon Football Practice facility features four lighted full-length fields and is located adjacent to the indoor practice facility. LSU is one of only a handful of schools with a full 100-yard indoor climate-controlled practice facility.

Dr. Martin Broussard Center For Athletic Training:

One of the largest and most complete of its kind at the collegiate level. Some of the features of the center include an on-site x-ray room, an in-house pharmacy and several hydrotherapy pools to treat ailing players.

Weightroom:

Measuring 10,000 square feet, the LSU weightroom features the latest in both strength and cardio-vascular training equipment. It is considered one of the finest in the SEC.

The Lawton Squad Room

Seating for 140 athletes inside a theater-like atmosphere is ideal for squad briefings.

The Captain's Lounge

An area where student-athletes can relax prior to team meetings. The lounge is equipped with a 72-inch TV, computer workstations and a billiards table.

The Hall of Champions

Features a wall honoring LSU alumni in the NFL, paintings of the Fighting Tiger All-Americans by former Tiger standout and accomplished international artist, Jack Jaubert, along with a tribute commemorating LSU's storied bowl game history.

9   Great Coaches

Charles Coates – In 1893 Coates founded the team. Hall in quadrangle commemorates his innovative career.

Edward Wingar – In two seasons Wingar went 17-2 (.850). He was 10-0 in 1908, and led LSU to the SIAA (Southern Intercollegiate Athletic Association) Championship.

Gaynell Tinsley – A two-time All-American end for the Tigers in 1935 and 1936, the Haynesville native led LSU to three straight conference titles. He is widely considered to be one of the toughest football players to ever play at LSU. A two-way starter, Tinsley was drafted in the second round of the 1937 NFL draft and later returned to Baton Rouge to coach from 1948-1954. His 1948 Tiger team finished 8-3 on the season with a number nine national ranking.

Paul Dietzel – "Pepsodent" Paul was 31 years old when he took over the LSU Football program in 1955. Prior to coaching in Baton Rouge, from 1942-1943 Dietzel served in the Army Air Forces as a pilot where he reached the rank of lieutenant and earned the Air Medal with clusters and a Presidential citation. A Duke University attendee and Miami of Ohio graduate, his Tigers would become the 1958 National Champions, LSU's first during college football's modern era. Often forgotten is that Dietzel's team nearly repeated as champions in 1959, losing only to Tennessee on a questionable call. He is remembered for his coaching genius that produced a platooning system, allowing him to play 35 to 40 players each game, keeping them fresh. Dietzel later served as head football coach and athletic director at South Carolina, from 1966 to 1974. He returned to Baton Rouge as LSU as athletic director from 1978 to 1982. Today, Paul Dietzel, the artist, lives in Baton Rouge where he enjoys painting as much or more as he once did coaching college football. Dietzel is trustee and past president of the American Football Coaches Association and was the 1958 National Coach of the Year.

*Paul
Dietzel*

Charles McClendon – By posting winning records in 16 of 18 seasons, from 1962 to 1979, "Cholly Mac" became LSU's most successful football coach, with an all-time record of 137-59-7. A native of Lewisville, Arkansas, McClendon played under Bear Bryant at Kentucky. His first coaching job was as an assistant at Vanderbilt in 1952. In 1953 he landed an assistant position at LSU under Coach Gaynell Tinsley, and later helped Paul Dietzel win a national championship in 1958 before taking over as head coach of the Bayou Bengals in 1961. Despite McClendon's success he was berated constantly by Tiger fans for failing to defeat more often his famed mentor, Paul "Bear" Bryant. Nevertheless, McClendon led LSU to two Sugar Bowls, two Cotton Bowls, two Bluebonnet Bowls, two Orange Bowls, two Sun Bowls a Tangerine Bowl, a Liberty Bowl and a Peach Bowl. Moreover, his 13 bowl appearances and seven bowl victories are school records. Fifteen of his eighteen seasons finished with squads ranked in the AP Top 15. In 1970, McClendon was named National Coach of the Year. He died December 6, 2001. The practice facility at LSU was named after him in September of 2002.

*Charles
McClendon*

Jerry Stovall – After finishing second in the Heisman balloting and a standout NFL career with the St. Louis Cardinals, Jerry Stovall eventually returned to LSU, as an assistant for head coach Charles McClendon. Stovall became LSU's head coach as an emergency hire in 1980, after new head coach Bo Rein died when his plane mysteriously depressurized and disappeared over the Atlantic Ocean. Thus, Stovall had the tall task of following in the footsteps of LSU's winningest football coach. With a 22-21-2 overall record at LSU in four years from 1980-1983, Stovall had an up-and-down tenure, finishing 7-4, 3-7-1, 8-3-1, and 4-7, respectively. Only one of Stovall's teams appeared in the final AP poll: the 1982 team. That team finished the season ranked #11 after it beat #4 Florida, #8 Alabama (Bear) and #7 Florida State (Bobby Bowden) and earned a spot in the Orange Bowl where LSU lost 21-20 to a #3 Nebraska team (Tom Osborne). As a result, in 1982, Stovall was named the National Coach of the Year by the Walter Camp Football Foundation.

Jerry Stovall

Bill Arnsparger – Arnsparger's hiring by athletic director Bob Brodhead in 1984 breathed a healthy dose of fresh air into the LSU athletic program. A former professional coach with the Miami Dolphins, each of Arnsparger's Tiger teams at LSU played in bowl games. Unfortunately, all three post-season games, two of which were against Nebraska, turned out to be losses. In three seasons Arnsparger guided the Tigers to a 26-8-2 record. His 1986 team finished 9-3 overall and 5-1 in the SEC to win the conference.

Arnsparger succeeded on the field but he did not possess the political clout necessary to keep his job. He left LSU after the 1986 season and took the athletic director's job at the University of Florida. It was in that capacity that Arnsparger would later hire a young football coach from Duke University, Steve Spurrier, the SEC's most successful modern-day coach.

*Bill
Arnsparger*

Mike Archer – In 1987, 31-year old Mike Archer–the youngest Division I head coach in America–took over for Bill Arnsparger in Baton Rouge. He coached four years at LSU, posting a respectable 27-18-1 (.598) record during that span. A Miami, Florida, native and a 1976 graduate of the University of Miami, Archer was a star defensive back and punter for the Hurricanes. Archer coached seven years as a secondary coach at Miami under Coach Howard Schnellenberger. In 1984, Archer left Miami to become the LSU defensive coordinator. After LSU, Archer assistant coached at Virginia for two seasons and at Kentucky for three before spending seven years with the Pittsburgh Steelers as their linebackers coach. Today, Archer is again the defensive coordinator for the Kentucky Wildcats, a position he has held since 2002. Archer's first two years at LSU were memorable. In 1987, the Tigers finished in the top ten with a 10-1-1 record. It was LSU's first 10-win season in more than 25 years. Archer followed it up with an SEC Championship in 1988, and an 8-4 record. The season was also famous for the "Earthquake Game" a 7-6 home victory over when Tiger fans so shook the stadium that the tremors registered on the seismograph in the nearby Geology Department.

*Mike
Archer*

Gerry DiNardo – In 1995, former All-American offensive lineman Gerry DiNardo embraced LSU during a down time in its storied football history. Following Curley Hudson Hallman's four-year tenure in which he notched a disappointing 16-28 record, DiNardo came to Baton Rouge from Vanderbilt and Colorado to bring respectability to the once-great program. A graduate of Notre Dame and a Brooklyn native, DiNardo won early with Curley Hallman's recruits and a few blue chippers of his own—like Kevin Faulk—but during his last two seasons in Baton Rouge his luck and his talent ran out. In five seasons DiNardo posted a more than respectable 32-24-1 (.570) record at the helm for the Tigers, with his biggest win coming in October, 1997 when LSU defeated Steve Spurrier's number one-ranked Florida Gators in an unlikely 28-21 upset in Tiger Stadium. After a short and unsuccessful stint as a head coach in the failed XFL pro league, DiNardo took the head coaching job at Indiana University in 2002, a post he left after two years. Today he is college game day football analyst for ESPN and ESPN radio.

*Gerry
DiNardo*

Nick Saban – In late 1999, prior to the 2000 football season, Nick Saban was named the 12th LSU head football coach and the school's 31st overall. Saban succeeded interim head coach Hal Hunter, who took over for a fired Gerry DiNardo. A graduate of Kent State where he was a 3-year letterman as a defensive back, Saban paid his dues by assistant coaching (defensive backs) at his alma mater under Don James, briefly at Syracuse, West Virginia, and for Earl Bruce at Ohio State. In 1983 Saban went to Michigan State and served as defensive coordinator under George Perles for five seasons. In 1988 and 1989 Saban coached the secondary for the Houston Oilers. Saban assumed his first head coaching position at Toledo in 1990, producing a 9-2 record. In 1991, Saban returned to the NFL for four seasons as Cleveland's defensive coordinator, making the Cleveland Browns' defense one of the NFL's best stop units. In 1995, Saban took the head coaching job at Michigan State where he coached for five seasons, ending with a best 9-2 record in 1999. In his first year in Baton Rouge the defensive-minded Saban went 8-4, culminating with a 28-14 victory over Georgia Tech in the Peach Bowl. In 2001, Saban built on his earlier success by leading LSU to its first SEC Championship since 1988 with a climactic come-from-behind victory over the Tennessee Volunteers in the SEC Championship Game. In 2002, LSU finished as SEC Western Division Co-Champs and in 2003 LSU repeated as SEC Champions with a decisive 34-13 victory over Georgia and Mark Richt. Saban went on later that year to defeat Oklahoma 21-14 in the Sugar Bowl in New Orleans for the BCS National Championship, LSU's first since 1958. After a 9-3 2004 season, Saban left LSU for the Miami Dolphins. Two years later Saban surprised the Tiger nation when he took the Alabama coaching job, after saying repeatedly that he was not interested.

Nick Saban

*Les
Miles*

Les Miles – Les Miles, a Michigan graduate, enjoys the lofty distinction of having the best start of any LSU coach in the program's storied history. Miles' 22 wins during his first two seasons is a school record, as are his back-to-back 11-win campaigns. Moreover, he was the first SEC coach in history to lead his team to the SEC title game during his first season. Considered a gentleman by his players and peers for his stoic demeanor and thoughtful presence, Miles has served the LSU program and university well on and off the field.

Prior to arriving at LSU Miles was the head coach of Oklahoma State for four years, leading them to an unprecedented three straight bowl games during that span. Before that he was an assistant with the Dallas Cowboys for three years. Furthermore, leading to Dallas he was an assistant at Oklahoma State, Michigan and Colorado.

In 2005 Miles took over the LSU Football Program as its 32nd coach in the catastrophic wake of two of the nation's most destructive hurricanes. Despite the monumental storm distractions, the first year coach led his team to a remarkable 11-2 record, with a triumphant 40-3 Peach Bowl victory over a 9th-ranked Miami Hurricane team. The only setbacks during that tumultuous inaugural season came against Tennessee at home and against Georgia in the SEC Championship.

The 2006 season was equally successful win-wise for Miles and the Tigers. After dropping tough road games against top-five ranked Auburn and Florida, LSU reeled off seven straight victories to finish the season with an identical 11-2 record, punctuated by a 41-14 drubbing of 11th-ranked Notre Dame in the Sugar Bowl in the New Orleans Superdome. Ironically, the 2007 Sugar Bowl was the first one played in the indoor arena since the 2005 hurricanes ravaged the Crescent City.

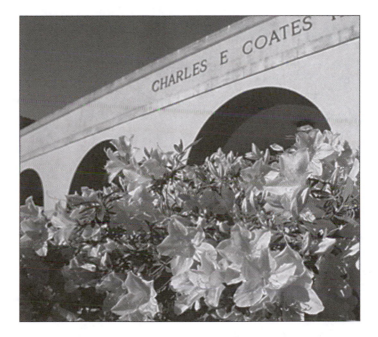

10   **Great Players**

Y.A. Tittle – The Marshall, Texas, native named Yelverton Abraham originally committed to play for the University of Texas. However, after a dorm visit in Austin from LSU assistant coach Red Swanson, Tittle packed his bags and headed to Baton Rouge. Capitalizing on his exceptional athleticism, Tittle led the Tigers to their first win over Alabama in thirty years, bringing national acclaim to LSU. A four-year starter at quarterback from 1944-1947, Tittle completed his college eligibility as the Tigers' all-time leading passer. After an illustrious pro career with the New York Giants, during which time he was twice selected as the NFL MVP—in 1957 and 1962—Tittle was inducted to the National Football League Hall of Fame in Canton, Ohio. Interestingly, Tittle's older brother attended Tulane and it was during a visit to the LSU campus by a younger Y.A. to watch LSU and Tulane play football that he first saw the beauty of the LSU campus. Oddly, Tulane never recruited Tittle, much to the chagrin of his older brother.

Y.A. Tittle

Billy Cannon – From 1957 to 1959 the Istrouma High (Baton Rouge) product's powerful legs led the Tigers to their first national championship in 1958. Known for his overall toughness and resolve, William Abb "Billy" Cannon possessed unparalleled rushing skills. Gifted with brute strength and sprinter speed, he was the prototypical running back during an era that had few sprinters. In his prime Cannon could run a legitimate 4.5 forty yard dash and a 9.5 hundred yard dash. His eternal run into Bengal Tiger and Southern college football lore came during the 1959 season when he returned a punt 89 yards against Ole Miss–breaking seven tackles along the way–to catapult the Tigers to a stunning 7-3 victory. For his remarkable gridiron accomplishments Cannon was named the 1959 Heisman Trophy recipient. At LSU Cannon rushed for 1,867 yards on 359 carries for a 5.2 yards per carry average. After college Cannon went on to a successful 11-year professional career. He was drafted #1 overall in 1960 by the Houston Oilers.

*Billy
Cannon*

Tommy Casanova – Known for his versatility, Casanova played on both sides of the ball as a running back, kick returner and safety during his three-time All-American LSU career. He is considered by many to be LSU's greatest football player. Precluded from playing football as a true freshman due to NCAA rules, Casanova was perhaps precluded from becoming an unprecedented, four-time All-American. Renowned as a fearless competitor both on and off the field, he remains one of seven three-time, First Team All-Conference players at LSU. From 1969-1971 he intercepted seven passes, rushed for 302 yards on 72 carries, returned 44 punts for 517 yards and returned 17 kickoffs for 334 yards. After LSU Casanova was drafted the 29th overall pick in the NFL draft. He played six seasons for the Cincinnati Bengals as a defensive back, where he was thrice named to the Pro Bowl. Today, the former State Senator Casanova is a medical doctor in his hometown of Crowley, Louisiana. In 1995 he was named to the National Foundation Football Hall of Fame in South Bend, Indiana.

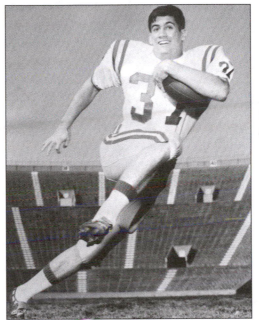

*Tommy
Casanova*

Ken Kavanaugh, Sr. – A superb athlete, Kavanaugh lettered in baseball and briefly played in the pros. An end, he scored all four touchdowns in a 28-7 victory over Holy Cross in 1939. He lettered from 1937-1939 and was a two-time All-SEC selection by the *Associated Press*. He finished seventh in 1939 Heisman balloting and he went on to an outstanding pro career with the New York Giants. After his pro playing days he worked as a scout for New York. His son, Ken, Jr., lettered as a receiver for three years at LSU from 1969-1971. During his college career the Little Rock native caught 58 passes for 1,075 yards and 17 touchdowns, remarkable totals during a day in which passing was not nearly as popular as it is today as a means for moving the ball.

Ken Kavanaugh, Sr.

George Tarasovic – A junior college transfer, Tarasovic was selected an All-American (*National Editorial Alliance*) and All-SEC player during his playing days at LSU. The Bridgeport, Connecticut native was a great all-around athlete and a standout center for the Tigers in 1951. His college career was abbreviated however due to his military service in the Korean conflict. Nevertheless, Tarasovic continued his football career after the Korean War by playing in both the NFL and AFL (Pittsburgh, Philadelphia and Denver) organizations as a linebacker for fifteen years. In 1952 he was drafted by the Steelers as the 18th pick in the second round of the NFL draft.

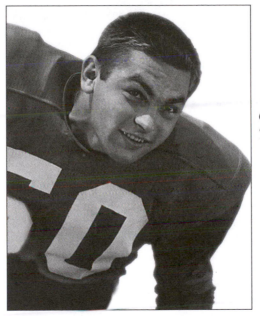

George Tarasovic

Jimmy Taylor – A hard-nosed fullback for the Tigers during the 1956 and 1957 seasons, after a brief stint at Hinds Community College, Taylor forged a reputation as a complete football player. He was a 1957 *Football Writers Association* All-American and was named the Most Valuable Player of the 1958 Senior Bowl. Taylor's pro career was legendary with the Green Bay Packers and he was inducted into the Pro Football Hall of Fame in 1976. He played with the Packers from 1958 to 1966 and with the New Orleans Saints in 1967. In 1962 he was named by the Associated Press as the NFL's Most Valuable Player. He is a member of the Louisiana Sports Hall of Fame and the LSU Athletic Hall of Fame. Today he lives in his hometown of Baton Rouge, Louisiana.

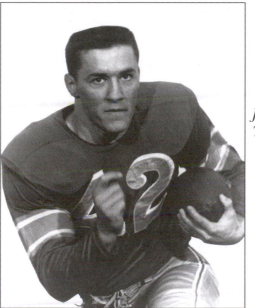

*Jimmy
Taylor*

Jerry Stovall – A favorite son of LSU, the 1962 consensus (*Associated Press, UPI, National Editorial Alliance, Central Press, Football Writers Association of America, Kodak/American Football Coaches Association, New York Daily News, The Sporting News, Time & CBS*) All-American halfback was ironically the last person recruited in his class by LSU. A West Monroe, Louisiana native, Stovall was runner-up in Heisman balloting in 1962 and was a First-Team All-SEC performer in 1961 by UPI and in 1962 by both AP and UPI. After LSU he played nine seasons with the St. Louis Cardinals (2nd pick overall in the 1963 NFL draft) as a defensive back before becoming an assistant coach at South Carolina. He returned to LSU as an assistant coach and was named head coach of the Tigers after the tragic death of Coach Bo Rein in 1980. He took LSU to the 1983 Orange Bowl and was named National Coach of the Year by the Walter Camp Football Foundation after the 1982 season.

*Jerry
Stovall*

Bert Jones – An All-American quarterback and standout signal caller for the Bayou Bengals during the early 1970's, Jones reportedly had as strong an arm as any quarterback in the history of the college game. During his senior year (1972), LSU went 9-2-1. Except for one week, LSU spent that entire season ranked in the Associated Press Top 10. That same year, Jones became the first quarterback in LSU history to be awarded consensus All-American honors. Nicknamed the "Cajun Cannon," Jones's right arm led the Tigers to a career record of 26-6-1. Moreover, he played in three bowl games and won the SEC title during his sophomore year. Jones is best remembered for his 28-8 victory over Notre Dame in 1971 and over Ole Miss in 1972 when, with time expired, he threw a touchdown pass to Brad Davis, giving his team and improbable 17-16 victory. The Ruston, Louisiana native was chosen as the second pick in the 1973 NFL draft by the Baltimore Colts. He played with Baltimore from 1973-1981 and with Los Angeles in 1982. In 1976, he was named to the Pro Bowl and was the NFL's Most Valuable Player.

*Bert
Jones*

Tommy Hodson – LSU's all-time leading passer in terms of yardage, Hodson, who wore number thirteen, was a rare All-SEC performer for four years (1986-1989) in Baton Rouge. Hodson led LSU to two Southeastern Conference Championships, first as a freshman in 1986 and then as a junior in 1988. As a freshman he led the Tigers in upset wins over two Top-Ten teams–Texas A&M (#7) and Alabama (#6). During his stellar career in Tiger Town the fan favorite completed 674 passes on 1,163 attempts for 9,115 total yards (SEC career best at the time) for a .579 completion percentage and 69 touchdowns. Hodson is LSU's only four-time First Team SEC Performer. He passed for over 2,000 yards during each of his four seasons at LSU, becoming only the 3rd player in collegiate history to achieve that feat. After LSU he was drafted 59th overall in the 1990 draft, and was the 3rd quarterback chosen by the New England Patriots. He played for three seasons with the Pats and also played briefly with Miami, Dallas and the New Orleans Saints. Today, the Matthews, Louisiana native works as a financial consultant in Baton Rouge with two other former LSU quarterbacks, Jessie Daigle and Mickey Guidry.

*Tommy
Hodson*

Kevin Faulk – From humble Cajun beginnings the gifted Kevin Faulk built himself through hard work and dedication into a complete football player. Along the way he attended LSU and completely rewrote the school and SEC record books. The versatile four-year starter (1995-1998) for the Tigers was an All-American all-purpose player in 1996 as a sophomore and he remains the school's all-time rusher as well as the SEC's all-time leader in all-purpose yardage totals (7,005 and 53 touchdowns) ahead of Bo Jackson and Herschel Walker. His all-purpose yardage totals are 5th in NCAA history. At LSU Faulk, the three-time All-SEC back, rushed for 5.3 yards per carry and 46 touchdowns. The Carencro native finished his career second on the all-time SEC rushing list behind Georgia great Herschel Walker (5,259 in 33 games). Faulk averaged 20.9 carries and 112 yards rushing per game for a total of 4,557, including 22 100-yard rushing games (LSU record). He was taken as the 46th pick in the second round of the 1999 NFL draft by the New England Patriots and has won three Super Bowl rings since as a third down back and special teams player. An outstanding student, Faulk impressively graduated from LSU in three and a half years with a B average.

*Kevin
Faulk*

Gabe Northern – A Baton Rouge native, Northern attended Glen Oaks High School where he honed his abundance of football talent before attending college. Northern signed with LSU in 1991 under Coach Curley Hallman's #1-ranked recruiting class. An aggressive defensive end, Northern was one of the best pass rushers to ever wear the purple and gold. An All-SEC performer and SEC Good Works team member in 1994 and 1995, Northern terrorized opposing quarterbacks with a blend of superior quickness, toughness and supreme upper body strength. His 21 career sacks rank third on the all-time list behind Ron Sancho (23) and Rydell Melancon (25). In 1994 Northern had 11 sacks, one shy of Oliver Lawrence's school season mark. His 37-yard fumble return for a touchdown in the 1995 Independence Bowl remains an Indy Bowl record. After LSU Northern played in the 1996 Senior Bowl in Mobile and professionally for the Buffalo Bills and the Minnesota Vikings.

Gabe Northern

Doug Moreau – As a split end for the Tigers during the mid-1960's Moreau was a sure-handed receiver and place kicker for the Tigers. During his junior season in Baton Rouge his trusty toe spurred the Bayou Bengals to their first two victories on the year—a 9-6 victory over Texas A&M and a 3-0 triumph over Rice. A First-Team All-American in 1964, the Baton Rouge native went on to the NFL after LSU, where he played for the Miami Dolphins. After pro football he earned a law degree. Today he serves as District Attorney for East Baton Rouge Parish and he is also the color analyst opposite Jim Hawthorne for the LSU football broadcasts on the *LSU Sports Network*.

*Doug
Moreau*

George Bevan – Considered by many to be the finest all-around linebacker ever to play at LSU. Although undersized, Bevan's persevering play never indicated it. A fierce competitor and natural leader, Bevan overcame a terrible Achilles tendon injury during his junior year to return and star for the Tigers. In 1969, after 32 months on crutches the Baton Rouge native shocked his doctors, teammates and coaches and made it back onto the field where he earned consensus (*Football Writers Association of America, Kodak/American Football Association*) All-American honors. Although he had many successful Tiger outings, he is perhaps best remembered for his blocked extra point against Auburn in the classic 21-20 Tiger victory. After his football playing days were over Bevan earned a law degree at LSU and is today a practicing attorney in Baton Rouge.

*George
Bevan*

Warren Capone – One of the better linebackers ever produced by LSU, Capone is another among a long line of Baton Rouge natives to star for the Bayou Bengals. A rare two-time All-American (*Football Writers Association, Kodak/American Football Coaches Association*) backer in 1972 and 1973, the hard-nosed Capone played in the Sun, Bluebonnet and Orange Bowls during his time with LSU. A widely heralded defensive player, Capone went on to play professionally with Birmingham in the short-lived World Football League and with the Dallas Cowboys of the NFL. While in Dallas he played in the Super Bowl with Alabama linebacking legend LeRoy Jordan. Capone is a past president of the National "L" Club. Today he lives in Baton Rouge, Louisiana where he is the head football coach of Christian Life Academy.

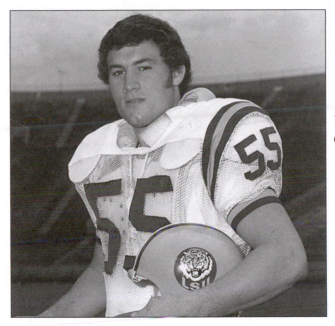

*Warren
Capone*

Mike Anderson – The 1970 unanimous All-SEC and First Team All-American (*UPI, Central Press, Football Writers Association, Kodak, Football News, Time,* etc.) linebacker started every game during his three-year Tiger career. The Baton Rouge native was the second of three straight All-American backers for LSU (Bevan, Anderson, Capone). Anderson is known best for his play against Auburn in 1970. LSU led 17-9. Auburn rushed 6-2, 225-pound fullback Wallace Clark on fourth and one inch. Anderson met him head-on to force Auburn to turn the ball over on downs. Anderson today owns a popular restaurant that bears his name off of Lee Drive near the LSU campus in Baton Rouge.

*Mike
Anderson*

Charles Alexander – During his illustrious Tiger career (1975-78) the Galveston, Texas native set nine SEC records, tied one and set an amazing 27 LSU marks. The two-time (1977, 1978) unanimous All-American (*Kodak/American Football Coaches, Football Writers Association, Walter Camp, Sporting News & The National Editorial Alliance*) and All-SEC running back rushed for 330 yards in the two bowl games he played in for LSU. Alexander still holds records for the most rushes in a game (43), most yards in a season (1686), most yards gained per game in a season (153.3), and most touchdowns in a season (17). In 1977, Alexander had 1766 all-purpose yards, for a 5.5 yards per play average. For his career Alexander had 4,513 all-purpose yards for a 5.0 yard per play average on 907 total plays. After his LSU days, Alexander was drafted in the first round by Cincinnati and played in the Super Bowl.

*Charles
Alexander*

Tyler Lafauci – During his three-year career the New Orleans native helped the Tigers to a 27-8-1 mark. Lafauci was involved in three bowl games, winning one (Sun) and dropping two (Bluebonnet & Orange). Although he was vertically challenged, Lafauci did not let his size affect his play. Fiercely competitive, the former All-SEC and All-American (*AP, UPI, Walter Camp, National Editorial Alliance*, 1973) player excelled at both run and pass-blocking. Lafauci was equally adept in the classroom. He went on to post-graduate work after LSU undergrad and earned a physical therapist degree. Today, he is a practicing physical therapist in Baton Rouge.

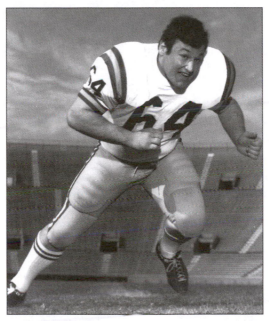

*Tyler
Lafauci*

Albert Richardson – The Baton Rouge native holds the LSU record for the most tackles recorded in a single game by a defensive player. A standout linebacker, Richardson logged an amazing 21 stops against Atlantic Coast Conference school, South Carolina, which is now a member of the SEC (1990). Richardson also holds the LSU record for the most tackles in a career, with 454. The four-year starter logged 150 tackles in 1981–a school record that lasted 21 years until Bradie James came along. A First-Team All-SEC and All-American (*UPI*) in 1982, Richardson was a tackling machine during his LSU days. From 1979 to 1982 he notched a phenomenal 54, 129, 150, and 121 take-downs respectively, nine career sacks, and five interceptions in four years.

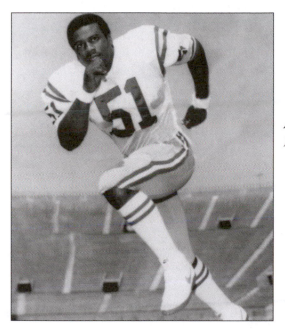

*Albert
Richardson*

Eric Martin – The Van Vleck, Texas native was a converted running back that turned out to be one of LSU and the conference's greatest receivers. At one point during his career Martin was the school leader in career receptions (105), in a season (52), receiving yards in a single game (209) and most receiving yards in a season (1064). The 1983 *Sporting News* All-American as a freshman was second in the nation in kickoff return yardage, including a 100-yarder for a touchdown against the Kentucky Wildcats. A two-time All-SEC performer in 1983 (*Associated Press*) and 1984 (*United Press International*), Martin caught 152 passes for 2625 yards and 14 touchdowns. From 1981 to 1984 he also rushed 8 times for 357 yards. Martin later played professionally with the New Orleans Saints.

*Eric
Martin*

Alan Faneca – A unanimous (*Associated Press, Football Writers Association of America, Walter Camp Foundation, The Football News & The Sporting News*) 1997 All-American selection at offensive guard, Faneca was largely responsible for LSU's riveting 28-21 victory over Steve Spurrier's Florida Gators in Baton Rouge. Quarterback Herb Tyler ran several times behind Faneca in that surprising win. A completely dominating blocker, Faneca was the first Outland Trophy finalist in LSU history and LSU's first winner of the Jacobs Trophy awarded to the best blocker in the SEC. The Rosenberg, Texas native (via New Orleans) anchored an effective offensive line from 1995 to 1997 that helped LSU lead the SEC in rushing for two straight seasons. Faneca, after allowing only one sack in 36 games started, left the college ranks early after his junior year and was the 26th pick of the first round of the NFL draft for the Pittsburgh Steelers, a team he still starts and stars for today. He has been to six Pro Bowls and has started five times.

*Alan
Faneca*

Wendell Davis – Number 82 is remembered well by Tiger fans as one of the school's most prolific receivers. A Shreveport native, Davis managed on twelve occasions 100 or more receiving yards. He finished his career (1984-87) with a then SEC record 2,708 yards receiving (Josh Reed). Davis currently ranks second in LSU history in receiving and sixth in league history. He also ranks among the top ten league totals in receiving yards during a single season (1,244), single season receptions, (80), and career receptions (183). A unanimous (*Football Writers Association, The Sporting News, Washington Post, College and Pro Football News Weekly, UPI, Kodak/American Football Coaches Association, Football News & Scripps-Howard News Service*), two-time All-American, Davis was a consensus all-conference player in 1987 and 1988, and was drafted by Chicago in the first round after his LSU playing days were over, spending five years with the Bears before tearing both ACL's, and effectively ending his career on the Houston Astrodome turf.

Wendell Davis

Chad Kessler – The Lake Mary, Florida native was a consensus (*Associated Press, American Football Coaches Association, The Football News, Walter Camp Foundation & The Sporting News*) All-American selection during the 1997 season. That year Kessler became the first player in college football history to average over 50.0 yards per punt for an entire season. Kessler was an All-SEC performer as a sophomore but had a quiet junior year. Kessler broke out during his final season as the nation's top punter. Also an excellent student, Kessler finished his student-athletic experience at LSU with an impressive 3.91 GPA. After college he initially pursued a professional career with Tampa Bay prior to opting for medical school. In 41 games Kessler punted 186 times for 7,976 yards (42.9 yards per punt average) and a career long punt of 66 yards.

*Chad
Kessler*

Michael Brooks – Considered to be one of the most aggressive and dominant linebackers in LSU's storied defensive history, Michael Brooks left an indelible impression on those that saw him play. Although he missed the final eight games of his college career, Brooks, a menacing Tiger linebacker, was a 1985 *Associated Press and Scripps-Howard News Service* All-American. The super athletic Ruston native was also selected as a consensus All-SEC performer that same year. In his four-year career for LSU Brooks recorded 206 tackles, 37 of which were behind the line of scrimmage. Brooks also recorded 20 sacks and 6 interceptions. Had he not injured his knee during the Florida game his senior season, he would have certainly been a two-time All-American pick. Prior to his injury, during the 1984 and 1985 seasons, Brooks made 150 tackles (75 twice). In 1987, he was drafted in the third round by the Denver Broncos organization.

*Michael
Brooks*

Greg Jackson – A 1988 *Gannett New Service* All-American, the Miami (Hileah), Florida native tied an NCAA record with a 100-yard interception return for a touchdown versus Mississippi State, and a 71-yard interception and return for a touchdown against arch-rival Tulane. Understandably, Jackson led the nation in 1988 in interception return yards with 219. That league mark has only been exceeded by Mississippi's Joe Brodsky's 244 yards in 1956. Jackson also returned 11 punts for the Tigers, gaining 99 yards during the 1988 season. Jackson made 199 tackles in four years and had 11 interceptions for 260 total return yards. An All-SEC performer during the 1988 season, Jackson was drafted at year's end by the New York Giants organization as the 78th pick in the third round. After a four year stint with the Giants Jackson played for Philadelphia for two years, the Saints for a year and San Diego for four.

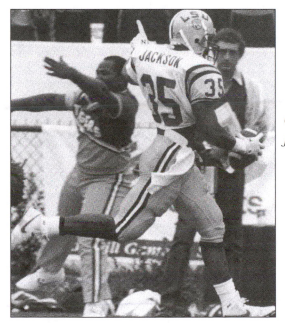

Greg Jackson

Nacho Albergamo – A consensus conference and All-American center in 1987, Albergamo was a fan favorite, much like his namesake. Nacho was the team's most heralded player during the 1987 season. Alongside Eric Andolsek, Albergamo comprised LSU's "A" Team which anchored the feared Tiger offensive line and helped pave the way to the school record total offense mark of 4,843 yards. A leader in the classroom as well, he was the 1987 Toyota "Leader of the Year." One of 11 recipients of the 1987 National Football Foundation and Hall of Fame Scholar Athlete Awards, he was twice named an Academic All-American. Today, the former unanimous All-SEC performer is now a medical doctor living in Baton Rouge.

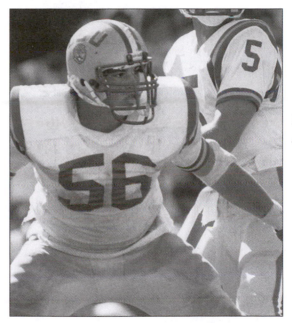

*Nacho
Albergamo*

Anthony "Booger" McFarland – A bullish defensive lineman for the Tigers from 1995 to 1998, the speedy, fan-favorite Winnsboro native was a four-year starter and a two-time All-SEC pick. As a true freshman Booger played in every game and even saw spot duty as a blocking fullback. Possessing unbelievable quickness for a player with his size, he was a terror for opposing offensive teams. Furthermore, his height of 6'1" made him a difficult blocking assignment. He finished his remarkable LSU career sixth on the all-time sack list with 17. Booger was a First-Team All-SEC performer his senior year, Second-Team All-SEC as a sophomore, the Defensive MVP in the 1996 Peach Bowl, and the SEC Freshman Co-Defensive Player of the Year in 1995. Also a First Team All-American (*Associated Press, The Football News*) and co-captain at LSU in 1998, Booger was a first round choice (15th) by the Tampa Bay Buccaneers in the 1999 NFL Draft. In 2006, Booger went to the Indianapolis Colts where he helped them win the Super Bowl.

*Anthony
"Booger"
McFarland*

Chad Lavalais – The Marksville native made an indelible mark during his playing days in Tiger land. A phenomenal senior season (2003) culminated in Southeastern Conference Defensive MVP and the *Sporting News* National Defensive Player of the Year honors while the Tigers won their second national championship in school history (1958). A consensus All-American, Lavalais used exceptional foot and hand speed to disarm and disrupt opponents with a relentless, speedy bull rush style. His standout play led a national championship defense that allowed only one team to score more than 20 points (Arkansas, 24) and only two teams to rush for over 100 yards. His play helped LSU lead the nation in scoring defense in 2003, with a 10.8 points per game scoring average. He was drafted in the sixth round of the NFL draft. While he waited to gain academic eligibility to attend LSU, Lavalais worked as a prison guard at a correctional facility near his hometown.

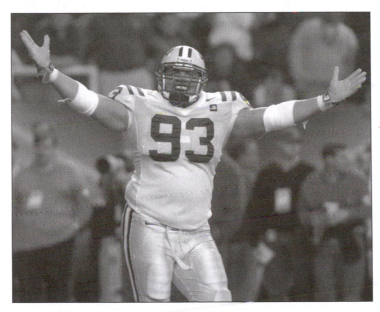

*Chad
Lavalais*

Josh Reed – A Rayne, Louisiana, native, Reed is one of the most decorated players in school history. During his brief gridiron career Reed completely rewrote the LSU and SEC record books for receiving. The 2001 Biletnikoff Award winner and a consensus All-American, Reed proved to be one of the best deep threats the conference ever produced. Despite starting only 15 of 31 games he played in for the Tigers, Reed hauled in 167 passes for 3,001 yards (18.0 yard per catch) and 17 touchdowns, becoming the first player in conference history to gain over 3,000 yards receiving in a career. In all, Reed set a total of 12 school and conference records. His 18 100-yard performances during his LSU career is a school record, and he is joined by Tennessee's Joey Kent (1995-96) as the only player in Southeastern Conference history to gain over 1,000 yards receiving in consecutive seasons. Reed was a first round choice by the Buffalo Bills in the 2002 NFL draft.

*Josh
Reed*

Stephen Peterman – The Waveland, Mississippi native and St. Stanislaus product was originally recruited to play tight end for the Tigers. After switching briefly to defensive end Peterman finally settled in at offensive guard. A tough as nails competitor and natural leader, Peterman's intensity helped lead a 2003 Bowl Championship Series National Championship Tiger offensive line that paved the way for five different running backs. As a three-year starter with 29 starts in 48 games, he logged an astonishing 133 knockdowns and 24 pancake blocks in 950 offensive snaps for the Tigers. A consensus All-American, Peterman earned first team honors from *Sports Illustrated*, *The Sporting News* and ESPN.com. An adept run and pass blocker, he was drafted in the third round by Bill Parcells of the Dallas Cowboys in the 2004 NFL Draft.

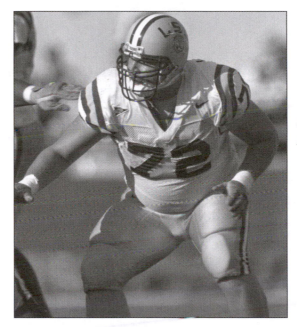

*Stephen
Peterman*

Rohan Davey – A Clarendon, Jamaica, native, Rohan Davey attended LSU via Miami Lakes, Florida, in 1998 and made his mark as one of LSU's all-time signal callers. A natural field general with exceptional leadership skills, Davey was known for his physical brand of play and his uncanny ability to throw on the run. Possessing a large frame, Davey was tough to bring down in the pocket and he had a rifle for an arm. During his senior season Davey used his unique talents to throw for an impressive 3,347 yards and 18 touchdowns, leading LSU to a 2001 SEC Championship in the process. In his Tiger career, Davey threw for 4,415 yards and 29 touchdowns with a .598 completion percentage (286 of 478). Davey was a fourth round (117) draft pick by the New England Patriots in 2002. He spent three years with the Patriots before transferring to the Berlin Thunder in the World League. In 2005 he played with the Arizona Cardinals and since 2006 has played in the Arena Football League with the New York Dragons.

Rohan Davey

Michael Clayton – A Baton Rouge native, Clayton is remembered as one of LSU's best all-around athletes. Clayton started 31 games during his three-year (2001-2003) career, leading LSU to two SEC Championships and a national championship en route. Amazingly, Clayton caught at least one pass in every game he played wearing an LSU uniform. In his career, Clayton caught 182 passes for 2,582 yards and 21 touchdowns. The 182 receptions ranks second in school history to Wendell Davis's 183 and the 21 touchdowns was a school record until Dwayne Bowe broke it in 2006. His 2,582 yards is 4th on the all-time LSU receiving yards list. Clayton ended his college career early by entering the 2004 NFL draft with one year of eligibility remaining. He was a first round draft choice (15th pick overall) of the Tampa Bay Buccaneers. During his 2004 rookie campaign with Tampa Bay, Clayton led all NFL rookies and the Buccaneers with 80 receptions for 1193 yards, and his team with 7 touchdowns.

Michael Clayton

Matt Mauck – The Jasper, Indiana, native spurred the Tigers to a huge upset victory over the 2nd ranked Tennessee Volunteers in the 2001 SEC Championship Game during his non-traditional freshman season. A former professional baseball player, Mauck was 22 when he made an impromptu appearance and earned MVP honors in the 2001 SEC Championship Game. Remembered for his ability to make plays with his feet and for his ability to read defenses, Mauck earned the starting job in 2002. In 2003 he led LSU to its first National Championship in 45 years in a 21-14 victory over Oklahoma in the Sugar Bowl at the New Orleans Superdome. Mauck threw for 2,825 yards and 28 touchdowns during his last year in an LSU uniform. His 18-2 record as a starter is the best winning percentage for an LSU quarterback. Like Clayton, Mauck decided to forego his senior season of eligibility at LSU to enter the 2004 NFL draft. He was a fourth round choice of the Denver Broncos.

Matt Mauck

Bradie James – A native of West Monroe, Louisiana, James, who wore number eleven, is remembered as a quintessential team leader and a sure tackler. A dominating linebacker that demanded great respect from his opponents, James played in 10 games as a true freshman for LSU. A physical player, he started every remaining game of his stellar four-year career, logging an impressive 248 solo tackles and 170 assists (418 total) in the process. He was only the second player in LSU history to log over 400 tackles (Al Richardson). A two-time All-SEC performer in 2001 and 2002, James became the first back-to-back all-conference linebacker for LSU since Warren Capone. With 154 tackles in 2002, Team Captain James became LSU's single-season record holder. After graduation the First Team All-American (*Sporting News, American Football Coaches Association, CBS Sportsline*) was drafted in the fourth round (103rd overall) by the Dallas Cowboys in the 2003 NFL draft.

*Bradie
James*

Domanick Davis – A dynamic back, Davis finished his quiet career at LSU second in school history and third in league history in all-purpose yards with 5,743 total yards (Kevin Faulk). The powerfully athletic Cajun running back and return specialist ranks second in SEC history with 95 career kickoff returns and ninth in punt returns with 94. In all, Davis had 30-100 yard all-purpose games. The Breaux Bridge, Louisiana, native was the fourth pick of the fourth round of the 2003 NFL draft. During his rookie season with the Houston Texans Davis (Williams) rushed for 1,031 yards, and in doing so earned Runner-up NFL Rookie of the Year honors and Diet Pepsi Rookie of the Year honors. Davis played running back for the Texans for four years (2003-2006) before he was released due to a devastating knee injury. He is the Houston Texans all-time leading rusher with 3,195 yards. After he left LSU, Domanick changed his last name to Williams, which he claims is his real last name.

*Domanick
Davis*

Donnie Jones – The standout punter from Catholic High School in Baton Rouge played in 50 games and will forever be remembered for his punt on the final play of the Tigers' win over Oklahoma in the National Championship game in the New Orleans Superdome. He punted more times for LSU than any other punter in history—233, and averaged 42.1 yards per punt, which is second in school history. Jones booted 12 punts of 50 yards or better during his senior season, including a best of 67 yards against the Auburn Tigers. On November 9, 2002, during his junior season against Kentucky, Jones set a Commonwealth Stadium record with a punt of 87 yards in what has been tabbed as the "Bluegrass Miracle" game (M. Randall to D. Henderson).

*Donnie
Jones*

Eric Edwards – The tall, tough Monroe, Louisiana, native played in 46 games and started 24 times during his career for the Bengal Tigers. After a redshirt freshman season that saw him catch five passes for 128 yards and two touchdowns, he still had to wait until he was a junior to get his first start. Edwards' career best game was a five-catch game against South Carolina in 2003. A member of the Tigers' second National Championship team (2003), Edwards is remembered as an intimidating presence on the Tiger offensive line as well as a talented tight end. He signed a free agent NFL contract with the Arizona Cardinals after the 2004 draft and later was picked up by the Washington Redskins.

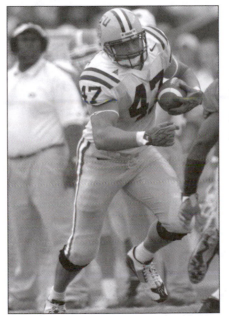

*Eric
Edwards*

Randall "Blue" Gay – A versatile member of the 2003 National Championship team, the standout cornerback and nickel back from nearby Brusly, Louisiana, played in 41 games for the Tigers and notched 16 starts. In his freshman season, Gay was one of seven newcomers to see playing time. He played extensively during the 2001 Sugar Bowl victory over Illinois. Originally tabbed as a running back, he suffered a broken arm early in 2003 that kept him out of the first two games of the season. During his Tiger career he posted 122 total tackles and two interceptions. In his junior season he started in all but one game and recorded 64 tackles, 46 of which were solo. After LSU, Gay signed a NFL free agent contract with the New England Patriots. Later he beat out starter Christian Morton and started and starred in Super Bowl XXXIX, resulting in a Patriot victory.

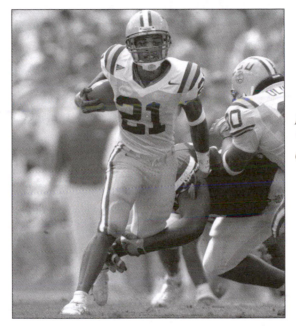

*Randall
"Blue"
Gay*

Jack Hunt – The Ruston, Louisiana, native played in 47 games with 20 starts. His first start came in 2002 against Kentucky, a game in which he posted a career-high 15 tackles. A pivotal member of the 2003 National Championship team, the athletic senior strong safety was the quarterback of the nation's best defense, calling for their proper alignments before each snap. Hunt was so valuable to the Tigers that they lost the only game of the season that he missed due to an MCL injury—the Florida game in Baton Rouge. In that game, the Gators exploited the vacuum left in Hunt's absence in the middle of the field. During his senior season Hunt recorded all four of his career interceptions. He finished with 131 career tackles for the Tigers.

*Jack
Hunt*

Marquise Hill – The New Orleans native played in 38 games with 25 starts during his abbreviated Tiger career. In his 3 playing years Hill notched 108 tackles, 17 of which were for losses totaling 74 yards. A towering figure at 6-7, 295 pounds, Hill was an intimidating bookend, complementing Marcus Spears on the Tigers' 2003 National Championship team. He started all 14 games that year for the Tigers, tallying 40 stops during the magical season. Many publications listed Hill as the nation's best defensive end coming out of high school. After choosing to go pro after his championship junior year, Hill reconsidered and attempted unsuccessfully to withdraw his name from the NFL draft. He was a second round pick by New England in the 2004 draft. In late May, 2007, Hill died in a jet ski accident. He was 24.

Marquise Hill

Rodney Reed – The West Monroe native was the Valedictorian of his West Monroe High School class. Known for his heady play and for his leadership ability, Reed excelled for the Tigers as an otherwise undersized offensive tackle. During the Tigers's meteoric run to the Sugar Bowl in 2003, Reed amazingly failed to allow a single sack of quarterback Matt Mauck in 916 snaps. Reed was a leader not only on the field, but also in the classroom, where he was twice named an Academic All-American (2002, 2003). He and Nacho Albergamo are the only Tiger players to ever be named a two-time Academic All-Americans. Reed was also a member of the *SEC Good Works Team* and a four-time member of the *SEC All-Academic Team*. After LSU, Reed signed a free agent contract with the Atlanta Falcons.

Rodney Reed

Joseph Addai – From 2001-2005 the Houston, Texas, native and former high school All-American proved to be one of the Tigers most reliable and tough runners. Addai played in 51 games with 19 starts in his LSU stint, piling up 2,577 rushing yards (5th in school history) during that span. He also proved himself adept at catching passes with 66, also 5th-best in LSU history among backs. His 490 rushing attempts rank 8th on the all-time LSU tally. Overall, the Sharpstown High graduate scored a total of 23 touchdowns, 18 rushing and 5 receiving, during his impressive Tiger career. After a standout 2006 Senior Bowl performance, Addai was drafted in the first round (30th) by the Indianapolis Colts organization. As a rookie, Addai rushed 226 times for 1081 yards, helping Peyton Manning and the Colts to a 2007 Super Bowl victory.

Joseph Addai

Andrew Whitworth – The West Monroe native set a school record from 2002-2005, starting 52 straight games in four straight years, and never missing a practice. At 6'7", 325 pounds, the steady Whitworth was an imposing, dominating presence on the LSU offensive line at left tackle, opening many holes for Tiger running backs during his outstanding Tiger career. A contributing member of the 2003 national championship squad, his 52 consecutive starts ranks just one behind the national record set by Derrick Strait of Oklahoma. A two-time consensus All-SEC player, Whitworth was a 2nd-Team Walter Camp All-American in 2005. In 2006 he was drafted by the Cincinnati Bengals in the 2nd round (55th pick overall).

*Andrew
Whitworth*

11 FIRST TEAM ALL-AMERICANS

(In Alphabetical Order)

Nacho Albergamo, Center, 1987
Charles Alexander, Tailback, 1977, 1978
Mike Anderson, Linebacker, 1970
George Bevan, Linebacker, 1969
James Britt, Cornerback, 1982
Michael Brooks, Linebacker, 1985
Billy Cannon, Halfback, 1958, 1959
Warren Capone, Linebacker, 1972, 1973
Tommy Casanova, Safety, 1969, 1970, 1971
Wendell Davis, Split End, 1986, 1987
Robert Dugas, Offensive Tackle, 1978
Ronnie Estay, Tackle, 1971

Alan Faneca, Offensive Guard, 1997
Kevin Faulk, All-Purpose, 1996
Sid Fournet, Tackle, 1954
Max Fugler, Center, 1958
John Garlington, End, 1967
Greg Jackson, Safety, 1988
Bradie James, Linebacker, 2002
Ken Kavanaugh, Sr., End, 1939
Chad Kessler, Punter, 1997
Tyler LaFauci, Guard, 1973
David LaFleur, Tight End, 1996
Chad Lavalais, Defensive Tackle, 2003
Todd McClure, Center, 1998
Anthony McFarland, Noseguard, 1998
Eric Martin, Split End, 1965
Fred Miller, Tackle, 1962

Doug Moreau, End, 1965
Stephen Peterman, Guard, 2003
Remi Prudhomme, Tackle, 1964
Josh Reed, Wide Receiver, 2001
George Rice, Tackle, 1965
Albert Richardson, Linebacker, 1982
Lance Smith, Offensive Tackle, 1984
Marvin "Moose" Stewart, Center, 1935, 1936
Jerry Stovall, Halfback, 1962
George Tarasovic, Center, 1951
Jimmy Taylor, Fullback, 1957
Gaynell "Gus" Tinsley, End, 1935, 1936
Billy Truax, End, 1963
Corey Webster, Cornerback, 2003
Mike Williams, Cornerback, 1974
Roy "Moonie" Winston, Guard, 1961
    (45 First Team All-Americans)

12   **Tiger Stadium**

Named for the team's mascot, the arena is also known as "Death Valley" to LSU opponents. East Stadium was constructed in 1926; West in 1932; North in 1937; South in 1957; and an addition was completed above the West side in 1978. The 2001 football season saw Tiger Stadium's already large capacity expand to 92,400, making it the fifth-largest on-campus stadium in America.

1. Michigan – (Michigan Stadium) 107,501
2. Penn State – (Beaver) 106,537
3. Tennessee – (Neyland) 104,079
4. Ohio State – (Ohio) 101,568
5. Georgia – (Sanford) 92,746
6. LSU – (Tiger) 92,400

Given Tiger Stadium's great fan capacity, on selected fall Saturdays it becomes more populous than 50 of the state's 64 parishes (counties). One of LSU and Tiger Stadium's greatest benefactors was Huey Pierce Long, the former demagogue governor who served from 1928-1932. A native Louisianian, Huey wanted LSU to have a bowl stadium, and a winning football program like the other national football powers of the day. However, university officials said what LSU really needed at the time was a dormitory. The clever Huey soon learned that the federal government would pay for classrooms and dorms through the Works Progress Administration. Long sought and discovered an architect who would design a stadium with dorms in it. Tiger Stadium dorms were still being used into the 1990's.

Tiger Stadium

Sport magazine has called Tiger Stadium in Baton Rouge: *"The most-feared road playing site in America."*

Coach Paul "Bear" Bryant of Alabama once remarked on the experience of Tiger Stadium: *"Baton Rouge happens to be the worst place in the world to be a visiting team. It's a dugout arena, and you get all of that noise. It's like being inside of a drum."*

On Tiger Stadium, legendary Coach Bobby Dodd of Georgia Tech once stated: *"I'd rather face the lions in the Coliseum than the Tigers in Baton Rouge."*

"Chance of rain…NEVER!"

– Tiger Stadium announcer Dan Borné

"Unbelievable, crazy! That place makes Notre Dame look like Romper Room!"

– Brad Budde, former Southern Cal
All-American

13

Tiger Stadium
Official Alcohol Policy

"The possession or consumption of alcohol in Tiger Stadium is expressly prohibited by University policy. Stadium personnel will enforce this policy. In an effort to encourage an enjoyable experience for all fans in Tiger Stadium, persons who are intoxicated or who are in possession of alcohol will be removed from the stadium."

14 Top 10 Tiger Stadium Crowds

1.	92,664	Auburn	Oct. 22, 2005	LSU	20-17 (OT)
2.	92,402	Florida	Oct. 15, 2005	LSU	21-17
3.	92,251	Georgia	Sept. 20, 2003	LSU	17-10
4.	92,213	Arkansas	Nov. 28, 2003	LSU	55-24
5.	92,141	Auburn	Dec. 1, 2001	LSU	27-14
6.	92,127	Arkansas	Nov. 25, 2005	LSU	19-17
7.	92,085	Auburn	Oct. 25, 2003	LSU	31-7
8.	92,077	Florida	Oct. 11, 2003	FL	19-17
9.	92,012	Alabama	Nov. 16, 2002	AL	31-0
10.	92,010	Florida	Oct. 6, 2001	FL	44-15

15 2006 National Attendance Figures

1. Michigan   7 games   776,405   110,915 average

2. Tennessee*   6 games   645,558   107,593 average

3. Ohio State   7 games   735,120   105,017 average

4. Penn State   7 games   734,013   104,859 average

5. Georgia*   6 games   556,206   92,701 average

6. LSU*   6 games   549,480   91,580 average

* For the 26th straight season, the SEC recorded the largest total attendance figure of any conference in the nation. In 2006, a total of 6,568,867 fans attended 87 games, an average of 75,504 per contest, also tops in the nation. SEC stadiums were filled to 96.48 percent of capacity for each home game in 2006.

16 The Golden Band From Tigerland

The LSU band has a colorful history. In 1893, inspired by the U.S. military, LSU established its own 11-person Cadet Band. By 1900 the Cadet Band became a marching unit. Tours throughout Louisiana and appearances at New Orleans Mardi Gras celebrations became early traditions. In 1924, the band made its first halftime appearance in Tiger Stadium. By the 1930's, Governor Huey P. Long took a personal interest in the LSU band, charting it on a unique course toward national prominence. Long co-wrote several songs for the band, including "Touchdown for LSU," still the predominant song featured in LSU's pregame show. Wanting the band to be second to none, the governor imported Castro Carazo, orchestra leader at the New Orleans Roosevelt Hotel, as the new bandmaster. Long even had the band exchange its traditional military dress for a showier stadium look.

Today, the Tiger Band consists of 325 musicians, the Golden Girls, and the Color Guard. The "halftime ballet corps" made their stadium debut in the 1950's and were briefly known as the "Dancing Football Team." By the 1960's, the squad was renamed the *Golden Girls*. The Tiger Band is one of the most uniquely important symbols of LSU's indomitable pride and tradition. Before each home football game, hundreds of LSU fans crowd the area near the Greek Amphitheater to listen to the Tiger Band warm up to a series of trumpet blasts and harmonies. As kickoff nears, thousands anxiously await the arrival of the Tiger Band inside the stadium to ignite the crowd as the Tigers ceremoniously take the field. In 2002, the John Phillip Sousa Foundation awarded the LSU Tiger Marching Band the 2002 Sudler Trophy, the highest honor a college marching band can receive.

17 LSU Songs

Fight Song: FIGHT FOR LSU!

Like Knights of old, Let's fight to hold
The glory of the Purple Gold.
Let's carry through, Let's die or do
To win the game for dear old LSU.
Keep trying for that high score;
Come on and fight,
We want some more, some more.
Come on you Tigers, Fight! Fight! Fight!
For dear old L-S-U. RAH!

Hey, Fightin' Tigers!
(Adapted from the original composition "Hey Look Me Over")

Hey, Fightin' Tigers, fight all the way
Play Fightin' Tigers, win the game today.
You've got the know how,
You're doing fine,
Hang on to the ball as you hit the wall
And smash right through the line
You've got to go for a touchdown
Run up the score.
Make Mike the Tiger stand up and roar.
ROAR!
Give it all of your might as you fight tonight
And keep the goal in view.
Victory for L-S-U!

Touchdown For LSU!

Tigers! Tigers! They've come to town,
They fight! They fight! Call a first down,
Just look them over, and how they can go,
Smashing the line with runs and passes
High and low.

Touchdown! Touchdown! It's Tigers' score.
Give them hell and a little bit more.
Come on you Tigers, Fight them, you
Tigers!
Touchdown for LSU.
Rah! U. Rah!

Tiger Rag (Hold That Tiger)

Long ago, way down in the jungle
Someone got an inspiration for a tune,
And that jingle brought from the jungle
Became famous might soon.
Thrills and chills it sends thru you!
Hot! So hot, it burns you too!
Tho' it's just the growl of the tiger
It was written in a syncopated way,
More and more they howl for the "Tiger"
Ev'ry where you go today
They're shoutin'
Where's that Tiger! Where's that Tiger!
Where's that Tiger! Where's that Tiger!
Hold that Tiger! Hold that Tiger!
Hold that Tiger!

18

Alma Mater.

By Lloyd Funchess and Harris Downey

Where stately oaks and broad magnolias shade
   inspiring halls,
There stands our dear old Alma Mater to who us recalls,
Fond memories that waken in our hearts a tender glow
And make us happy for the love that we have
   learned to know,
All praise to thee, our Alma Mater, molder of mankind,
May greater glory, love unending, be forever thine.
Our worth in life will be thy worth, we pray to keep it true,
And may thy spirit live in us, forever LSU.

19   Campus Landmarks

The Campanile – Often referred to as "the tower" or "the clock or bell tower" is the obelisk memorial granted by the students and the people of Louisiana to those who lost their lives during World War I. A clock at the top of the tower once chimed, however today it is silent. The bottom of the tower houses a working museum. Legend has it that if an LSU coed kisses her "beau" at the strike of midnight in front of the bell tower then he is the one that she'll marry. Many LSU married couples claim to have engaged in this age-old campus tradition and ritual.

*The
Bell
Tower*

Indian Mounds. Since 1926 LSU has existed at its present location off of Highland Road. While the campus has seen many changes and additions, the Indian mounds, located on the northwest side of campus, have remained in their natural state. During the 1980's, LSU scientists took soil samples from the mounds and discovered that they are part of a group of archaic mound complexes found throughout Louisiana. These mound groups are older than any in North America, Mesoamerica, and South America, and predate the construction of the great Egyptian pyramids. Built more than 5,000 years ago by Native Americans, the mounds have varied significance. Archaeologists think the Native American mounds served as ceremonial and social centers. The structures do not appear to have been burial places, temples or houses. Researchers believe they may have been symbols of group identity where peoples living in scattered bands congregated periodically for religious and ceremonial purposes, and to feast, dance, exchange information, and select mates. Currently, the structures and artifacts within the mounds are protected from vandals and treasure hunters. In 1999, the LSU Indian Mounds were listed on the National Register of Historic Places.

The Pete Maravich Assembly Center – Named for the greatest scorer in the history of men's college basketball, Peter Press Maravich. Maravich scored 3,667 points during his three-year career at LSU, averaging an amazing 44.2 points per game. The indoor arena that bears his name was built in the early 1970's. The spaceship-like structure's architecture is its most renowned feature. Unbeknownst to many basketball fans is that an entire practice gymnasium known as "the dungeon" exists beneath the hardwood surface of the Maravich Assembly Center. This auxiliary gym allows for the basketball team to practice while other sports are using the Assembly Center floor.

*Pete
Maravich
Assembly
Center*

20 Restaurants

The Chimes – 3357 Highland Road at the North Gates of the LSU campus. This twice-renovated drugstore adjacent to the Varsity has some of the best food in town at great prices. Also, there are plenty of good beers on tap. Open seven days a week.

(225) 383-1754

Mike Anderson's Seafood – 1031 West Lee Drive. Anderson played for LSU where he was an All-American linebacker in 1970. If you like fried and boiled seafood, this is the place. Adult beverages available at the inside bar and on the Side Porch.

(225) 766-7823

Ruffino's – If you love authentic Italian food in a fine dining atmosphere you won't want to pass this one up. Partly-owned and operated by former Tiger offensive lineman Ruffin Rodrigue, this is a sure-fire palate-pleaser. Located off of I-10 headed East to New Orleans. Formerly DiNardo's Restaurant.

(225) 753-3458

George's – A South Baton Rouge favorite, Smokie's place is your call if you like great burgers, fried seafood, cold beers and a laid-back atmosphere. Located on Highland Road just minutes from the LSU campus.

(225) 768-8899

Brunet's Cajun Restaurant – 135 S. Flannery Road. Bob and his brother Billy have been in the restaurant business for over 30 years. Bob played for Louisiana Tech and later for the Washington Redskins. Authentic Cajun food is served daily and live Cajun music and dancing is featured every Wednesday and Saturday

(225)-272-6226

Walk-Ons Bistreaux & Bar– LSU's newest tradition. Located near the intersection of Nicholson Drive and Burbank Ave. within view of Tiger Stadium. A popular meeting place for students, alumni and faculty. Opened by two former LSU basketball walk-ons, it has numerous TV's, many beers on tap and a great socializing atmosphere.

(225) 757-8010

Rocco's New Orleans Style Poboys: Drusilla Lane. Let Troy and Bert whip you up a New Orleans style original! The Smokin' Bert's Hot Sausage is to die for. Or, if you like a sloppy Roast Beef, give it a try. The Gumbo, or anything else catered by Chef Jeff is excellent, (225) 248-9999 or for catering,

(225) 248-9903

The Silver Moon Café: Chimes Street. Mama's famous soul food recipes are as wicked as Bourbon Street voodoo. Red beans and rice like you've never had before along with white beans, smothered chicken and spicy Southern spaghetti. Quite simply, if you've never done it, you ain't lived!

(225) 383-1754

Saloons

The Varsity Theatre: This refurbished old movie theater is a great venue for live music and retro dancing. Get in on the action after Tiger football games. Located on Highland Road near the North Gates of campus right next to The Chimes.

(225) 383-7018

Ivar's Sports Bar & Grill: Located at 2954 Perkins Road, underneath Interstate 10. Sample some of the best hot wings and whet your palate with plenty of ice cold beer. Rated the best sports bar in Baton Rouge.

(225) 388-0021

Fred's Bar & Grill: A long-standing Greek tradition. Great drink specials and live music on game weekends. Enjoy the laid-back atmosphere of the Sunset Club on the outside deck. 1184 Bob Pettit Dr.

(225) 766-3543

Zee Zee Gardens: Within walking distance of Ivar's, Zee Zee's always has a good thirty-something crowd. A local favorite to see and be seen. Located at the foot of the overpass. 2904 Perkins Rd.

(225) 346-1291

Buffalo Wild Wings: If you like big sports bars with plenty of TV's, darts, foosball and pool tables, this is your thing. 7524 Bluebonnet Drive.

(225) 819-8438

21 Famous/Distinguished Alumni

Hubert Humphrey (deceased)
Vice President of the United States (1964-68)

Carlos Roberto Flores
President of Honduras (1997 – present)

Lod Cook
Retired Chairman and CEO of ARCO

Max Faget
NASA Engineering & Development Director

Bill Conti
Academy Award Winner, Composer and
Conductor for "The Right Stuff"

Rex Reed
New York Author & Critic

Elizabeth Ashley
Actress with "Evening Shade"

Russell Long (deceased)
Former U.S. Senator, Chairman, Senate Finance Committee

Shaquille O'Neal
NBA Star, Actor, Entertainer

James Carville
Political Consultant, Commentator

John J. Lejeune
WWI Marine Corps Commandant, Camp "Lejeune," North Carolina

Gen. Claire Chennault
Founder and Commander of World Renowned "Flying Tigers"

Gen. Troy Middleton
8th Army Commander, held Bastogne during World War II Battle of the Bulge

D.M. Waghelstein
Operator, USMC Recon, USAF Pararescue, U.S. Special Operations

Kevin Griffin
Lead singer of the platinum-selling rock band "Better Than Ezra."

Walter Hitesman
Former President, *Reader's Digest.*

22   Traditions

Ole War Skule

LSU began in 1860 as the Louisiana State Seminary of Learning and Military Academy, shortly before the beginning of the Civil War. LSU's first superintendent was Civil War General William Tecumseh Sherman, who sided with the Union. Because of the school's rich military history, "Ole War Skule" was formerly a popular reference to LSU, as was the term, "Ole Lou."

Cheerleaders

LSU cheerleaders have long been a part of the game day experience. Pregame ceremonies feature the LSU Cheerleaders atop Mike the Tiger's cage as it circles the field. The cheerleaders also traditionally lead the Tigers onto the field before and at the half. The 1989 Tiger cheerleaders were named national champs at the annual Universal Cheerleading competition.

Tigers Invade Cuba

LSU was the first college team to play on foreign soil in 1907 when head coach Edgar Wingard traveled his Tigers to Havana to play. The University of Havana squad had dominated every American service team it had contested until the Tigers arrived. The agility of the Tiger team took the larger Cubans by surprise on Christmas Day at Almendares Park and LSU walked away with a unanimous 56-0 victory witnessed by 10,000 spectators.

Perfect Seasons:
1895 • 1896 • 1898 • 1905 • 1908 • 1958

LSU has had six unblemished seasons in its gridiron history. In 1895, Coach A.P. Simmons led the Tigers to a 3-0 record. The 1908 team, coached by Edgar Wingard, coasted through the 10-game schedule without a loss or a tie. Tiger standout Doc Fenton—a legendary player scored 125 points on the year. Fifty years later LSU won its first national championship, going 11-0.

The Kingfish

One of the most influential persons in the history of Louisiana State University, Huey Pierce Long left an indelible mark on the university and football program he worked so hard to empower. Long used his political clout as governor like no other in aiding the cause of the football team. In 1934, athletic director T.P. Heard reported low advance ticket sales for the impending LSU-SMU game due to a circus coming to town the night of the game. Long contacted Barnum & Bailey and informed them of an obscure Louisiana animal-dipping law. The show was abruptly canceled and LSU-SMU ticket sales skyrocketed. Later that year Long enticed passenger agents of the Illinois Central Railroad to lower fares for LSU students traveling to a Vanderbilt football game. After Long threatened to reassess the value of railroad bridges in the state from $100,000 to $4 million, the railroad agreed to give LSU students a $6 round trip fare for the game.

Huey
Pierce
Long

Stadium Dormitories

Tiger Stadium is unique in many ways. One feature that sets it apart from other venues is that it once housed some 1,500 dorm rooms, home to many LSU students. This idea was introduced by T.P. "Skipper" Heard, who is also credited for bringing night football to Tiger Stadium. Heard learned that LSU President James Smith proposed to use $250,000 to build new dormitories on the LSU campus. Heard persuaded Smith to raise the stands on both the East and West sides and extend them to the end zones. Dorms were then constructed inside the stadium. This expansion raised the stadium's capacity by 10,000 seats. This building phase occurred during the reign of Governor Huey Long, in 1931.

Night Football

Prior to the advent of electric lamps, college football was played during the day. The tradition of playing night games in Tiger Stadium began on October 3, 1931, when LSU defeated Spring Hill, 35-0, under the lights. Playing under the lights, according to Skipper Heard, the idea's master, helped threefold. 1) It avoided the heat and humidity of afternoon games, 2) It avoided scheduling conflicts with Loyola and Tulane, and 3) It gave fans busy tending to their plantations during the day an opportunity to watch LSU football. LSU traditionally plays better at night. Since 1960, LSU has won over 75% of its night games at home, compared to less than 50% of its day home contests.

A Jersey Numbering System

In 1952, LSU introduced a rare and short-lived numbering system. Spawned by head coach Gaynell Tinsley and publicity director Jim Corbett, the idea used an abbreviation system adorned on player's jerseys. Ends, guards and tackles wore "E", "G" and "T" followed by a single-digit number. The right side of the line wore even numbers, the left side odd numbers. Accordingly, centers, quarterbacks, left halfbacks, right halfbacks and fullbacks wore "C", "Q", "L", "R" and "F", respectively, followed by single-digit numbers. The 1953 LSU Yearbook, *The Gumbo*, boldly predicted that the new system would revolutionize college football jersey numbering. Of course, it did not.

The Chinese Bandits

The nickname of the three units used in Paul Dietzel's platoon system that helped the Tigers to the 1958 National Championship. The first team was named the White Team, an offensive unit was named the Go Team and a defensive unit was tabbed the Chinese Bandits. "Chinese Bandits" originated when Dietzel remembered a line from a comic strip that referred to the Bandits as "the most vicious people in the world." During their heyday, the Chinese Bandits were featured in Chinese masks in *Life* magazine. In 1980 the LSU band revived the custom of playing the "Bandit" tune when the LSU defense stalls any opponent drive.

89 Yards

There have been longer scoring runs in LSU football lore, however Billy Cannon's 89-yard punt return against Ole Miss in 1959 is undoubtedly the most famous play in school history. Some consider it the most significant play in college football history; and certainly in Southern football history. On a misty, Halloween night in Tiger Stadium, the Rebels took a 3-0 lead into the final quarter, trying to end LSU's 18-game win streak. On third and 17 from the Ole Miss 42, the Rebels' Jake Gibbs booted the ball 47 yards to the Tiger 11. Cannon caught the ball on the bounce and took off 89 yards into gridiron immortality. Cannon later won the *Heisman Trophy* for his game heroics.

All Hallow's Eve

Halloween drama between LSU and Ole Miss is as traditional as jack-o-lanterns and goblins. The two schools have met seven times on October 31st with the series tied 3-3-1. The first meeting between the two schools on Halloween was the famous 1959 contest that featured Billy Cannon's great punt return. In 1964, Ole Miss led 10-3 late in the game in Baton Rouge when LSU scored a touchdown to make it 10-9. Quarterback Billy Ezell threw to Doug Moreau in the front corner of the endzone on the conversion for an 11-10 win. There was a 17-year hiatus until the teams played again on Halloween. In 1981, in Jackson, a seesaw battle ended with a 46-yard LSU field goal to tie. Most recently, in 1998, Ole Miss won 37-31 in Oxford.

South End Zone Goal Line Stands

Many Tiger fans remember Billy Cannon's storied run into college football history. However, fewer recall that there was a goal line stand after the run that preserved the victory for the Tigers. The south end zone of Tiger Stadium has become a sort of Maginot line for the Tiger defense. During the past score of years Tiger defenders have affected eight goal line stands at the south end zone: 1985 Colorado State, 1985 Florida, 1986 North Carolina, 1986 Notre Dame, 1988 Texas A&M, 1991 Florida State, 1992 Mississippi State, and 1996 Vanderbilt. In 1988, the Tigers denied the Texas Aggies at the 2-yard line even with the distraction of a bank of lights going dim overhead. For that series LSU's defense earned the nickname "Lights Out Defense."

The Earthquake Game

Quarterback Tommy Hodson connected with wide receiver Eddie Fuller on his second try in the back of the north end zone for the touchdown that vaulted LSU to a 7-6 victory over the Auburn Tigers on October 8, 1988. The dramatic late game play gave the Tigers their seventh SEC crown, one they ironically had to share with the Plainsmen. The moment will forever be known as the "Night the Tigers Moved the Earth" as the play that caused such a thunderous explosion from the 79,341 fans in Tiger Stadium the LSU Geology Department registered vibrations on a seismograph machine at the exact instant the touchdown was scored.

Victory Hill

A pre-game ritual for many Tiger fans is the lining of North Stadium Drive during the hours before kickoff to see the Tiger Marching Band in its stroll from the band hall. The band pauses prior to each game on the hill next to the Journalism School to play "Tiger Rag" to the delight of the LSU faithful. During the early 1990's former head coach Curley Hallman began the tradition of walking the team down victory hill. Coaches Gerry DiNardo and Nick Saban continued the practice. The team stays in an on-campus hotel the night prior to the game and the team bus brings them to Broussard Athletic Hall instead of Tiger Stadium in order for the players to make their arrival down Victory Hill.

LSU vs. Tulane

LSU's first game in 1893 was played against Tulane. Given the popularity of football in Louisiana and the great pride shared by the fans of each school for their ball clubs, it is understandable that the contest developed into a great rivalry. Tulane won that inaugural game by the score of 34-0 but since that time LSU has gained the upper hand in the series with a favorable 65-22-7 tally. The 70 miles between the two schools at first was considered lengthy but by 1913 fans were using cars instead of the train to view the game. Today's Tiger fans can make it to the Superdome to watch the game in less than 90 minutes, but according to the *Times Picayune*, during the early days the trip was six hours.

The Crossbar

Unbeknownst to many Tiger fans is that the LSU football team runs onto the field under the same crossbar that was once part of the north end zone goalpost in Tiger Stadium as early as 1955. Running under the goalpost was already a tradition when the new "T-style" goalposts came into fashion. For the sake of tradition the old "H-style" goalposts stood on the field of Death Valley until it was finally removed in 1984. Part of the crossbar, however, was kept and fastened above the door of the Tiger Den through which the Tigers run onto the field each game. In 1993, as part of the centennial celebration of LSU football, the "H-style" goalpost was returned to the end zones of Tiger Stadium as a result of a corporate donation.

The Rag

The Rag was the banner that for many years signified the traditional spoils of victory between LSU and Tulane. A flag decorated half in LSU's colors of purple and gold, and half in the green and white of Tulane, it was held by the victor until the following season. A heated rivalry that was once tarnished by violence on and off the field, The Rag hoped to civilize the contest. The whereabouts of the original flag are unknown. However, a new version of The Rag was awarded to the LSU squad after the Tigers defeated the Green Wave 48-17 in the 2001 season opener in Death Valley, the last time the two teams have met on the gridiron.

Voice of the Tigers

For years John Ferguson was known as the "Voice of the Tigers." Ferguson's distinctive, booming voice was synonymous with Tiger football for years prior to the advent of often-televised games. The most famous radio call in history, however, belongs to J.C. Politz who was the "Voice of the Tigers" in 1959 when Billy Cannon made his famous 89-yard run. By the time Cannon reached midfield on that play a technician tried to increase the volume to raise it above the crowd noise. In his excitement, however, he turned the knob down instead of up. As a result, much of Politz's call was lost forever. Ferguson later returned as "The Voice," then moved into television where he worked on Tigervision broadcasts starting in 1984. At that time Jim Hawthorne assumed duty as "The Voice" and remains in that capacity today for not only football, but also for baseball and basketball.

23 Ten Great Years in LSU Football History

10. 1895 – Undefeated for the first time (2-0).

9. 1908 – 10-0. First 10-win season. SIAA champions.

8. 1935 – Biff Jones goes 9-2, wins first SEC crown.

7. 1946 – Bernie Moore goes 9-1-1, plays in Cotton Bowl.

6. 1958 – Dietzel goes 11-0, Sugar Bowl, National Champs.

5. 1961 – Paul goes 10-1, 6-0 in SEC, Co-Champs, Orange.

4. 1969 – McClendon goes 9-1, 4-1 in SEC (Ole Miss).

3. 1987 – Archer goes 10-1, (4th time) Mazda Gator Bowl.

2. 1997 – DiNardo goes 9-3, beats #1-ranked Florida.

1. 2003 – Saban goes 13-1, SEC and BCS National Champs.

24   SEC & National Championship Teams

1935 Bernie Moore, 9-2, 5-0 in SEC

1936 Bernie Moore, 9-1, 6-0 in SEC

1958 Paul Dietzel, 11-0, 6-0 in SEC (SEC, National)

1961 Paul Dietzel, 10-1, 6-0 in SEC (Co-Champs)

1970 Charles McClendon, 9-3, 5-0 in SEC

1986 Bill Arnsparger, 9-3, 5-1 in SEC

1988 Mike Archer, 8-4, 6-1 in SEC (Co-Champs)

2001 Nick Saban, 10-3, 5-3 in SEC

2003 Nick Saban, 13-1, 7-1 in SEC (SEC, National)

25 Current Players in the Pros

(35 as of 08/2006)

Joseph Addai	Indianapolis Colts
Eric Alexander	New England Patriots
Kenderick Allen	Green Bay Packers
Bennie Brazell	Cincinnati Bengals
Ryan Clark	Washington Redskins
Michael Clayton	Tampa Bay Buccaneers
Travis Daniels	Miami Dolphins
Domanick Davis	Houston Texans
Alan Faneca	Pittsburgh Steelers
Kevin Faulk	New England Patriots

Randall Gay	New England Patriots
Jarvis Green	New England Patriots
Skyler Green	Cincinnati Bengals
Devery Henderson	New Orleans Saints
Marquise Hill	New England Patriots
Bradie James	Dallas Cowboys
Tory James	Cincinnati Bengals
Eddie Kennison	Kansas City Chiefs
E.J. Kuale	New Orleans Saints
Nate Livings	Cincinnati Bengals
Matt Mauck	Tennessee Titans
Kevin Mawae	Tennessee Titans
Todd McClure	Atlanta Falcons

Anthony McFarland	Indianapolis Colts
Stephen Peterman	Detroit Lions
Josh Reed	Buffalo Bills
Mark Roman	San Francisco 49ers
Robert Royal	Buffalo Bills
Marcus Spears	Dallas Cowboys
LaBrandon Toefield	Jacksonville Jaguars
Cameron Vaughn	Denver Broncos
Corey Webster	New York Giants
Andrew Whitworth	Cincinnati Bengals
Kyle Williams	Buffalo Bills
Claude Wroten	St. Louis Rams

26 Radio Stations Carrying Tiger Football

Alexandria KFAD-FM 93.9 (6,000 Watts)
Alexandria KSYL-AM 970 (1,000 Watts)
Amite WTGG-FM 96.5 (6,000 Watts)
Baton Rouge WDGL-FM 98.1 (100,000 Watts)
Bogalusa WBOX-AM 920 (1,000 Watts)
Bogalusa WBOX-FM 92.9 (3,000 Watts)
Bunkie KEZP-FM 104.3 (18,000 Watts)
Eunice KEUN-AM 1290 (1,000 Watts)
Ferriday KFNV-FM 107.1 (18,500 Watts)
Folsom WJSH-FM 104.7 (6,000 Watts)
Hammond WFPR-AM 1400 (1,000 Watts)
Hammond WHMD-FM 107.1 (3,000 Watts)
Houma KCIL-FM 107.5 (100,000 Watts)

Jena KJNA-FM 102.7 (6,000 Watts)
Jennings KHLA-FM 92.9 (50,000 Watts)
Lafayette KVOL-FM 105.9 (6,000 Watts)
Lake Charles KLCL-AM 1470 (5,000 Watts)
Leesville KJAE-FM 92.7 FM (3,000 Watts)
Leesville KLLA-AM 1570 (1,000 Watts)
Many KWLV-FM 107.1 (25,000 Watts)
Marksville KAPB-FM 97.7 (3,000 Watts)
Minden KASO-FM 95.3 (5,000 Watts)
Monroe KLIP-FM 105.3 (25,000 Watts)
Moreauville KLIL-FM 92.1 (3,000 Watts)
Morgan City KFXY-AM 1490 (1,000 Watts)
Morgan City KBZZ-FM 96.7 (25,000 Watts)
Natchitoches KZBL-FM 95.9 (50,000 Watts)
New Iberia KANE-AM 1240 (1,000 Watts)
New Orleans WWL-AM 870 (50,000 Watts)
Opelousas KSLO-AM 1230 (1,000 Watts)
Ruston KPCH-FM 97.7 (50,000 Watts)

Shreveport KWKH-AM 1130 (50,000 Watts)
Slidell WSLA-AM 1560 (1,000 Watts)
Tallulah KBYO-AM 1360 (500 Watts)
Thibodaux KTIB-AM 640 (5,000 Watts)
Ville Platte KVPI-FM 93.5 (3,000 Watts)

Arkansas

Crossett KWLT-FM 102.7 (25,000 Watts)
Mississippi
McComb WHNY-AM 1250 (5,000 Watts)
Monticello WRQO-FM 102.1 (50,000 Watts)
Picayune WKSY-FM 106.1 (50,000 Watts)

Texas

Hemphill KTHP-FM 103.9 (6,000 Watts)

Satellite Radio

Selected games on Sirius

27 Schedules

2007

Aug. 30	at Mississippi State
Sept. 8	Virginia Tech
Sept. 15	Middle Tennessee
Sept. 22	South Carolina
Sept. 29	at Tulane
Oct. 6	Florida
Oct. 13	at Kentucky
Oct. 20	Auburn
Nov. 3	at Alabama
Nov. 10	Louisiana Tech
Nov. 17	at Ole Miss
Nov. 24	Arkansas

2008

Aug. 30	Troy State
Sept. 6	TBD
Sept. 13	TBD
Sept. 20	at Auburn
Sept. 27	Mississippi State
Oct. 11	at Florida
Oct. 18	at South Carolina
Oct. 25	Georgia
Nov. 1	Tulane
Nov. 15	Alabama
Nov. 22	Ole Miss
Nov. 29	at Arkansas

2009

Sept. 5	North Texas
Sept. 12	Vanderbilt
Sept. 19	Houston
Sept. 26	at Mississippi State
Oct. 3	at Georgia
Oct. 10	Florida
Oct. 24	Auburn
Oct. 31	at Tulane
Nov. 7	Southern Miss
Nov. 14	at Alabama
Nov. 21	at Ole Miss
Nov. 28	Arkansas

28 National, Conference, School Records

National Records Held by LSU Players

Punting: Chad Kessler – Highest Average Per Punt – Season 1997 – 50.3 yards per punt (39 punts for 1,961 yards)

Total Kick Returns: Pinky Rohm – Most Touchdowns Scored On Kick

Returns – Season; 1937 – 5 returns for touchdowns (3 punts, 2 kickoffs) Tied in 1997 by Robert Woods of Grambling

National Leaders
1939: Ken Kavanaugh, Receiving, 30 catches for 467 yards
1943: Steve Van Buren, Scoring, 98 points (14 TDs, 14 PAT)
1964: Doug Moreau, Field Goals, .650 (13 of 20)
2002: Josh Reed, Receiving, 145.0 yards per game (94 for 1,740)

SEC Records Held by LSU Players

Rushing

Yards Per Rush – Game (min. 10 rushes) 19.6
Harvey Williams, v. Rice, 1987 (196 yards, 10 att.)

All-Purpose Yards – Season, 2,109
Kevin Faulk, 1998 (1,279 rush, 287 rec., 265 PR, 278 KOR)

All-Purpose Yards – Season Average, 191.7 ypg
Kevin Faulk, 1998 (2,109 in 11 games)

All-Purpose Yards – Career, 6,833
Kevin Faulk, 1995-1998 (4,557 rush, 600 rec., 832 PR, 844 KOR)

Receiving Yards – Career, 3,001
Josh Reed, 1999-2001 (167 for 3,001)

Receiving Yards – Season, 1,740
Josh Reed, 2001 (94 for 1,740)

Receiving Yards – Game, 293
Josh Reed, 2001, versus Alabama

Receptions – Game, 19
Josh Reed, 2001, versus Alabama

Yards Per Catch – Season (Min. 50 catches) 20.5
Eric Martin, 1983 (52 for 1,064)

Yards Per Catch – Season (Min. 75 catches) 18.5
Josh Reed, 2001 (94 for 1,740)

Touchdown Catches – Game, 5
Carlos Carson v. Rice, 1977

Total Yards – Game, 540
Rohan Davey v. Alabama, 2001 (12 rush, 528 pass)

Scoring

Rushing Touchdowns – Season, 19
LaBrandon Toefield, 2001

Field Goal Percentage – Season (Min. 10 made), 100
David Browndyke, 1989 (14 of 14)

Most Points By Non-Kicker – Career, 318
Kevin Faulk, 1995-98 (46 rush, 4 rec, 2 PR, 1 KOR)

Punting

Punting Average – Season (Min. 30 Punts), 50.3
Chad Kessler, 1997 (39 for 1,961)

Punt Returns

Punt Return Touchdowns – Game, 2
Tommy Casanova v. Ole Miss, 1970 (Tied with 3 others)

Punt Return Touchdowns – Season, 3
Pinky Rohm, 1937 (Tied with 4 others)

Total Kick Returns

Kick Return Touchdowns – Season, 5
Pinky Rohm, 1937 (3 punts, 2 kickoffs)

29 SEC Annual Leaders from LSU

Rushing

(Based on per game average beginning in 1970)

1953 Jerry Marchand (137 for 696 yards)

1957 Jimmy Taylor, (162 for 767 yards)

1958 Billy Cannon (115 for 686)

1964 Don Schwab (160 for 683)

1976 Terry Robiskie (101.5, 224 for 1,117)

1977 Charles Alexander (153.3, 311 for 1,686)

1997 Kevin Faulk (127.1, 205 for 1,144)

1998 Kevin Faulk (116.3, 229 for 1,279)

Passing Efficiency

1971 Bert Jones, 141.43 (119 att, 66 cmp, 945 yards)

1972 Bert Jones, 129.00 (199 att, 103 cmp, 1,446 yards)

1982 Alan Risher, 146.00 (234 att, 149 cmp, 1,834 yards)

1986 Tommy Hodson 142.90 (288 att, 175 cmp, 2,261 yards)

1989 Tommy Hodson 143.41 (317 att, 183 cmp, 2,655 yards)

Receiving

(Based on receptions per game beginning in 1970)

1986 Wendell Davis, 7.3 (80 rec. for 1,244 yards)

1987 Wendell Davis, 6.6 (72 rec. for 993 yards)

1991 Todd Kinchen, 4.8 (53 rec. for 855 yards)

2001 Josh Reed, 7.83 (94 rec. for 1,740 yards)

Total Offense

(Based on avg. yards per game beginning in 1970)

1977 Charles Alexander, 162.1 (1,783 yards in 11 games)

1989 Tommy Hodson, 236.7 (2,604 yards in 11 games)

Scoring
(Based on points per game beginning in 1970)

1938 Pinky Rohm, 54 points

1943 Steve Van Buren, 98 points

1956 Jimmy Taylor, 59 points

1957 Jimmy Taylor, 86 points

1958 Billy Cannon, 74 points

1961 Wendell Harris, 94 points

1964 Doug Moreau, 73 points

1976 Terry Robiskie, 6.5, 72 points

1977 Charles Alexander, 9.5, 104 points

1997 Kevin Faulk, 10.0, 90 points

1998 Kevin Faulk, 9.27 102 points

Punting

1948 Rip Collins, 41.3

1967 Eddie Ray, 42.8

1987 Matt DeFrank, 41.6

1989 René Bourgeois, 43.9

1995 Chad Kessler, 44.1

1997 Chad Kessler, 50.3 (NCAA Record)

1999 Corey Gibbs, 43.02

LSU Career Rushing Leaders

Kevin Faulk (1995-98) (856 for 4,557) 5.3ypc 46 TDs

Dalton Hilliard (1982-85) (882 for 4,050) 4.6ypc 44 TDs

Charles Alexander (1975-78) (855 for 4,035) 4.7ypc 42 TDs

Harvey Williams (1986-1990) (588 for 2,860) 4.9ypc 27 TDs

Terry Robiskie (1973-76) (578 for 2,517) 4.4ypc 29 TDs

LaBrandon Toefield (2000-02) (511 for 2,291) 4.5ypc 26 TDs

Garry James (1982-85) (491 for 2,217) 4.5 ypc 27 TDs

Rondell Mealey (1996-99) (453 for 2,238) 4.9 ypc 29 TDs

Brad Davis (1972-74) (456 for 2,165) 4.8ypc 15 TDs

Domanick Davis (1999-2002) (455 for 2,056) 4.5 ypc 20 TDs

LSU Career Passing Leaders

1. Tommy Hodson (1986-89) (9,115 675-1,163) 58.0% 69 TDs

2. Jeff Wickersham (1982-85) (6,921 587-1,005) 58.4% 25 TDs

3. Jamie Howard (1992-95) (6,158 459-934) 49.1% 34 TDs

4. Herb Tyler (1995-98) (5,876 434-715) 60.7% 40 TDs

5. Alan Risher (1980-82) (4,585 381-615) 62.0% 31 TDs

LSU Career Receiving Leaders

1. Josh Reed (1999-2001) (3,001-167) 17.9 17 TDs

2. Wendell Davis (1984-87) (2,708-183) 14.8 19 TDs

3. Eric Martin (1981-84) (2,625-152) 17.3 14 TDs

4. Michael Clayton (2001-03) (2,582-182) 14.1 21TDs

5. Tony Moss (1986-89) (2,196-132) 16.6 16 TDs

30 1958 National Champions
11-0, 6-0

September 20	at Rice	W, 26-6
September 27	at Alabama	W, 13-3
October 4	Hardin-Simmons	W, 20-6
October 10	at Miami	W, 41-0
October 18	Kentucky	W, 32-7
October 25	Florida	W, 10-7
November 1	Ole Miss	W, 14-0
November 8	Duke	W, 50-18
November 15	at Mississippi State	W, 7-6
November 22	at Tulane	W, 62-0

Sugar Bowl, New Orleans, Louisiana
January 1, 1959
LSU 7, Clemson 0

31 2003 National Champions
13-1, 7-1

August 30	Louisiana-Monroe	W, 49-7
September 6	at Arizona	W, 59-13
September 13	Western Illinois	W, 35-7
September 20	Georgia	W, 17-10
September 27	at Mississippi State	W, 41-6
October 11	Florida	L, 7-19
October 18	at South Carolina	W, 33-7
October 25	Auburn	W, 31-7
November 1	Louisiana Tech	W, 49-10
November 15	at Alabama	W, 27-3
November 22	at Ole Miss	W, 17-14
November 28	Arkansas	W, 55-24

December 6 *SEC Championship Game* (Ga.) W, 34-13
January 4   S*ugar Bowl New Orleans Superdome* W, 21-14

32 Bowl Games Played

LSU has played in 38 bowl games (19-18-1)

Sugar Bowl (6-7)

Vs. TCU	2-3 Loss	January 1, 1936
Vs. Santa Clara	14-21 Loss	January 1, 1937
Vs. Santa Clara	0-6 Loss	January 1, 1938
Vs. Oklahoma	0-35 Loss	January 1, 1950
Vs. Clemson	7-0 Win (NC)	January 1, 1959
Vs. Ole Miss	0-21 Loss	January 1, 1960
Vs. Syracuse	13-10 Win	January 1, 1965
Vs. Wyoming	20-13 Win	January 1, 1968
Vs. Nebraska	10-28 Loss	January 1, 1985
Vs. Nebraska	15-30 Loss	January 1, 1987
Vs. Illinois	47-34 Win	January 1, 2000
Vs. Oklahoma	21-14 Win (NC)	January 4, 2004
Vs. Notre Dame	41-14 Win	January 3, 2007

Peach Bowl (4-0)

Vs. Florida State	31-27 Win	December 30, 1968
Vs. Clemson	10-7 Win	December 28, 1996
Vs. Georgia Tech	28-14 Win	December 29, 2000
Vs. Miami	40-3 Win	December 29, 2005

Independence Bowl (2-0)

| Vs. Michigan State | 45-26 Win | December 29, 1995 |
| Vs. Notre Dame | 27-9 Win | December 28, 1997 |

Cotton Bowl (2-1-1)

Vs. Arkansas	0-0 Tie	January 1, 1947
Vs. Texas	13-0 Win	January 1, 1963
Vs. Arkansas	14-7 Win	January 1, 1966
Vs. Texas	20-35 Loss	January 1, 2003

Orange Bowl (2-3)

Vs. Texas A&M	19-14 Win	January 1, 1944
Vs. Colorado	25-7 Win	January 1, 1962
Vs. Nebraska	12-17 Loss	January 1, 1971
Vs. Penn State	9-16 Loss	January 1, 1974
Vs. Nebraska	20-21 Loss	January 1, 1983

Sun (1-1)

Vs. Iowa State	33-15 Win	December 18, 1971
Vs. Stanford	14-24 Loss	December 31, 1977

Gator Bowl (1-0)

Vs. South Carolina	30-13 Win	December 31, 1987

Tangerine Bowl (1-0)

Vs. Wake Forest	34-10 Win	December 22, 1979

Hall of Fame Bowl (0-1)

| Vs. Syracuse | 10-23 Loss | January 2, 1989 |

Liberty Bowl (0-2)

| Vs. Missouri | 15-20 Loss | December 23, 1978 |
| Vs. Baylor | 7-21 Loss | December 27, 1985 |

Bluebonnet Bowl (0-2)

| Vs. Baylor | 7-14 Loss | December 21, 1963 |
| Vs. Tennessee | 17-24 Loss | December 30, 1972 |

Capital One Bowl (0-1) (Formerly Tangerine/Citrus)

| Vs. Iowa | 30-25 Loss | January 1, 2005 |

33 Coaches & Records

1893	Charles Coates (1-0) 1.00
1894-95	A.P. Simmons (5-1) .833
1896-97	A.W. Jeardeau (7-1) .875
1898	E.A. Chavanne (1-0) 1.00
1899	J.P. Gregg (1-4) .200
1900	E.A. Chavanne (2-2) .500
1901-03	W.S. Borland (15-7) .681
1904-06	D.A. Killian (8-6-2) .563
1907-08	Edgar Wingard (17-3) .850
1909	J.G. Pritchard (4-1) .800
1910	J.W. Mayhew (3-6) .333
1911-13	J.K. Dwyer (16-7-2) .680
1914-1916	E.T. McDonald (14-7-1) .659
1917	W.S. Sutton (3-5) .375
1918	No Games due to World War I –
1919	Irving R. Pray (6-2) .750

1920-1921	Branch Bocock (11-4-2) .706
1922	Irving R. Pray (3-7) .300
1923-1927	Mike Donahue (23-19-3) .544
1928-1931	Russ Cohen (23-13-1) .635
1932-1934	Biff Jones (20-5-6) .741
1935-1946	Bernie Moore (83-39-6) .671
1948-1954	Gaynell Tinsley (35-34-6) .507
1955-1961	Paul Dietzel (46-24-3) .651
1962-1979	Charlie McClendon (137-59-7) .692
1980-1983	Jerry Stovall (22-21-2) .511
1984-1986	Bill Arnsparger (26-8-2) .750
1987-1990	Mike Archer (27-28-1) .598
1991-1994	Curley Hallman (16-28) .364
1995-1999	Gerry DiNardo (32-24-1) .570
2000-2004	Nick Saban (48-16) .750
2005-2006	Les Miles (22-4) .846

2006 Overall School Record: 658-372-47
SEC Record: 267-188-22

34 Southeastern Conference Champions Since 1933

1933   Alabama (5-0-1)
1934   Tulane (8-0) & Alabama (7-0)
1935   LSU (5-0)
1936   LSU (6-0)
1937   Alabama (6-0)
1938   Tennessee (7-0)
1939   Tennessee (6-0), Georgia Tech (6-0) &
       Tulane (5-0)
1940   Tennessee (5-0)
1941   Mississippi State (4-0-1)
1942   Georgia (6-1)
1943   Georgia Tech (3-0)
1944   Georgia Tech (4-0)
1945   Alabama (6-0)

1946 Georgia (5-0)
1947 Mississippi (6-1)
1948 Georgia (6-0)
1949 Tulane (5-1)
1950 Kentucky (5-1)
1951 Georgia Tech (7-0) & Tennessee (5-0)
1952 Georgia Tech (6-0)
1953 Alabama (4-0-3)
1954 Mississippi (5-1)
1955 Mississippi (5-1)
1956 Tennessee (6-0)
1957 Auburn (7-0)
1958 LSU (6-0)
1959 Georgia (7-0)
1960 Mississippi (5-0-1)
1961 Alabama (7-0) & LSU (6-0)
1962 Mississippi (6-0)

1963	Mississippi (5-0-1)
1964	Alabama (8-0)
1965	Alabama (6-1-1)
1966	Alabama (6-0) & Georgia (6-0)
1967	Tennessee (6-0)
1968	Georgia (5-0-1)
1969	Tennessee (5-1)
1970	LSU (5-0)
1971	Alabama (7-0)
1972	Alabama (7-1)
1973	Alabama (8-0)
1974	Alabama (6-0)
1975	Alabama (6-0)
1976	Georgia (5-1)
1977	Alabama (7-0) & Kentucky (6-0)
1978	Alabama (6-0)
1979	Alabama (6-0)

1980 Georgia (6-0)
1981 Georgia (6-0) & Alabama (6-0)
1982 Georgia (6-0)
1983 Auburn (6-0)
1984 Florida (5-0-1)
1985 Florida (5-1) & Tennessee (5-1)
1986 LSU (5-1)
1987 Auburn (5-0-1)
1988 Auburn (6-1) & LSU (6-1)
1989 Alabama (6-1), Tennessee (6-1) &
       Auburn (6-1)
1990 Florida (6-1)
1991 Florida (7-0)

Championship Game

1992 Alabama 28, Florida 21
1993 Florida 28, Alabama 23
1994 Florida 24, Alabama 23
1995 Florida 34, Arkansas 3
1996 Florida 45, Alabama 30
1997 Tennessee 30, Auburn 29
1998 Tennessee 24, Mississippi State 14
1999 Alabama 34, Florida 7
2000 Florida 28, Auburn 6
2001 LSU 31, Tennessee 20
2002 Georgia 30, Arkansas 3
2003 LSU 34, Georgia 13
2004 Auburn 38, Tennessee 28
2005 Georgia 34, LSU 13
2006 Florida 38, Arkansas 28

Southeastern Conference College Football National Champions

(Year, Team, Poll[s])

1951 Tennessee, AP, UPI
1957 Auburn, AP
1958 LSU, AP, UPI
1960 Ole Miss, FWAA
1961 Alabama, AP, UPI
1964 Alabama, AP, UPI
1965 Alabama, AP, FWAA
1973 Alabama, UPI
1978 Alabama, AP, FWAA
1979 Alabama, AP, UPI, FWAA
1980 Georgia, AP, UPI, FWAA
1992 Alabama, AP, UPI, USA Today, FWAA
1996 Florida, AP, USA Today, FWAA
1998 Tennessee, AP, USA Today, FWAA
2003 LSU, USA Today/ESPN (BCS)
2006 Florida, USA Today/ESPN (BCS)

SEC Composite Bowl Record

(School, bowl record, bowl winning percentage)

Alabama 30-20-3 (.598)
Arkansas 11-21-3 (.348)
Auburn 18-13-2 (.580)
Florida 15-18 (.452)
Georgia 23-16-3 (.589)
Kentucky 6-5 (.545)
LSU 19-18-1 (.513)
Ole Miss 19-12 (.613)
Mississippi State 6-6 (.500)
South Carolina 4-9 (.307)
Tennessee (24-22) .521
Vanderbilt (1-1-1) .500

Overall (176-164-13) .517

35

NCAA All-Time Coaching Wins

1. John Gagliardi 443-120-11 (.781) 1949-2006
2. Eddie Robinson 408-165-15 (.707) 1941-1997
3. Bobby Bowden 366-113-4 (.764) 1959-2006
4. Joe Paterno 363-121-3 (.750) 1966-2006
5. Amos Alonzo Stagg 340-200-36 (.622) 1890-1946
6. Paul W. Bryant 323-85-17 (.780) 1945-1982
7. Glenn "Pop" Warner 318-107-32 (.731) 1895-1938
8. Roy Kidd 314-124-8 (.713) 1964-2002
9. Harold Raymond 300-119-3 (.714) 1966-2001

SEC All-Time Coaching Wins
Coach, School, Dates, SEC, Overall

1. Paul Bryant KY, 1946-53, UA, 1958-82, 159-46-9, 323-85-17
2. Johnny Vaught, OM, 1947-70, 106-41-10, 190-61-12
3. Vince Dooley, UGA, 1964-88, 105-41-4, 201-77-10
4. Shug Jordan, AU, 1951-75, 98-63-4, 175-83-6
5. Steve Spurrier, UF, 1989-2001, SC 2005-06, 90-26, 157-50-2
6. Phil Fulmer, UT, 1992-present, 90-28, 137-40
7. Wally Butts, UGA, 1939-60, 67-60-5, 140-86-9
8. Robert Neyland, UT, 1926-34, 36-40, 46-52, 62-15-5, 173-31-12
9. Charlie McClendon, LSU, 1962-1979, 62-38, 137-59-7
10. Frank Thomas, UA, 1931-46, 59-16-6, 115-24-7
11. Johnny Majors, UT, 1978-92, 57-40-3, 116-62-8

36   2007 Coaching Staff

Head Coach: Les Miles
(50-25 overall) (22-4 @LSU)
Birthday: November 10, 1953
Birthplace: Elyria, Ohio

Assistant Head Coach/Running Backs: Larry Porter
Wide Receivers/Passing Game: DJ McCarthy
Offensive Coordinator: Gary Crowton
Defensive Coordinator: Bo Pelini
Linebackers: Bradley Dale Peveto
Defensive Line: Earl Lane
Tight Ends: Josh Henson
Offensive Line: Greg Studrawa
Defensive Backs: Doug Mallory

37 Tailgating History

Tailgating—The Colorful History of America's Biggest Sporting Pastime

TAILGATING—ITS MERE MENTION among football fans conjures cool, leaf-blown images of the fall and football season. This widely anticipated weekend engagement is regularly staged against the inviting autumn backdrop of sexy young coeds, ice cold beer and of course, food. Ah yes—tailgating, the veritable game before the game, and for many football fans—the more important one, is today as much a feature of the modern football experience as the forward pass. This burgeoning American cultural phenomenon is ubiquitous, and it can be witnessed prior to kickoff in the parking lot of your favorite pro stadium or on the lazy, sprawling campus of your revered alma mater. Tailgating has grown in recent years into the quintessential culinary side show of the modern sporting era; a veritable Epicurean outdoor feast that regularly precedes the fall ritual of collegiate and pro football games. While modern tailgating has only recently (within the last thirty years) become popular, the practice of enjoying both food and football, has post-Civil War, nineteenth century roots.

Early Times

In the beginning, there was only college football. Professional football did not arrive on the American sporting scene until the 1950's, while the first college football game ironically occurred between Ivy League schools Rutgers and Princeton in New Brunswick as early as 1869. Twelve years later, in 1881, the first collegiate football game south of the Mason-Dixon Line occurred on the bluegrass at Old Stoll Field in Lexington, Kentucky. Even during the earliest days of the sport, food and football went hand in hand. In those days it was customary for the fans of each team to engage in a wild fish and game supper before the contest and then to revisit the leftovers after the game where they relived the on-field exploits of the daring young gridders.

Because of football's brutal nature it was a game at its onset played by only the toughest young men. Players in those days wore little protective equipment like that enjoyed by today's players. It was common instead for the young men to grow their hair long and wear it in a bun to cushion the fierce bodily contact that typified the game. Furthermore, the most common way of bringing down a ball carrier during football's late nineteenth century roots was to simply strike him in the face with a closed fist.

Amidst the painful aftermath of the bloody North-South conflict, college football quickly bore into the core of the American cultural psyche, especially in the South, where the game's mythical connections to the lost cause of the Confederacy of the Civil War were omnipresent. College football games for young men in the South after the Civil War presented an immediate opportunity for them to recapture the pride they had been stripped of in the bitter conflict. Furthermore, playing college football allowed young southern men to assert themselves well in a tough physical game and thereby again demonstrate their superiority over the North. In short, football, at the time, was a game that brought otherwise highly divergent national institutions like the North and the South together with a common purpose and point of cultural reference. However, football was not only a veritable rite of passage for the players, but also for their adoring fans, who saw winning football and its social trappings—the rudiments of tailgating, as the grand redeemer of a pride earlier lost.

And Then There Was Light

For years after the turn of the century up until the advent of electric lighting and night football during the late 1920s and early 1930s, college football games were played almost exclusively during the day. Towering electric lamps and night football games brought about the practice of hosting all day football parties at fans' homes where they would congregate and leisurely hop from house-to-house as the evening kickoff approached. Night games were a critical social development since they allowed for cooler game time temperatures and for men and women to dress up for the popular pre-game parties. Women commonly wore their best Sunday dresses adorned with team-colored corsages while men frequently donned spiffy coats, ties and the now-forgotten, but once-popular derbies and fedoras.

These festive pre-game jaunts continued unabated for forty years or more until daytime college football on television pre-empted the house parties that were previously the norm. Along with much-needed athletic department revenue, TV coverage also brought with it the dreaded day football games, which entirely precluded the practice of party hopping around town prior to the contest. The alternative to not house partying was simple to the legions of football fans that had been weaned on pre-game football parties: Take the party to the stadium! And that they did, because today tailgating at or near the stadium is a social practice that seems to have found a continual flow of willing fall participants. Predictably, tailgating now occurs regularly prior to night games and day games as college football's fan base—and their propensity to tailgate—only grows with each passing year. Tailgating has become so popular that some football fans enjoy it as much as the game itself—and that's saying something in the football-crazed American heartland!

One often-overlooked or under-studied aspect of tailgating is its name. Simple logic leads one to surmise that the term describes the practice of having an outdoor picnic on the tailgate of a truck or station wagon, and this is largely understood to be true. However, no official etymology of the American word exists, further reinforcing the fledgling status of this growing sporting tradition.

The "Commissioner" of Tailgating

There is perhaps no individual that can better explain the fascinating sociology of American tailgating than the self-proclaimed "Commissioner of Tailgating," Joe Cahn, of New Orleans, Louisiana. Although his dream job is a tough one, Cahn, over the past seven years has made a comprehensive national pilgrimage in his fully functional recreational vehicle to frequent the hottest tailgating locales the country has to offer. Now in his eighth season on the road, Cahn has amazingly steered his "Joemobile" over 217,000 miles, visited hundreds of venues and tailgated with thousands of hungry football fans. Like a nomad with a purpose, Cahn has burned nearly 35,000 gallons of gasoline during his journey to all 32 NFL stadiums and over 60 college stadiums across the nation. Along the way Joe has delighted his discriminating taste buds with delicacies like barbecue brisket in Dallas, grits in Atlanta, Bratwurst in Green Bay, cheesesteaks in Philly, smoked salmon in Seattle, boiled lobsters in New England, Jambalaya in Cajun country and Pierogi's in Pittsburgh, just to name a few.

Cahn, a tireless promoter of the pastime who also enjoys Dorito's as a corporate sponsor (somebody has to pay his gas bill!), claims that tailgating has taken the place of the State Fair and the forgotten front porch visit in Americana. Cahn, who also maintains an internet website dedicated to his cause (tailgating.com), contends that tailgating brings people together better than any other modern outdoor event.

"It (tailgating) is the new community social and the biggest weekly party in the nation! Tailgating is the last great American neighborhood—the Tailgating Neighborhood—where no one locks their doors, everyone is happy to see you and all are together sharing food and football. Tailgating is great because it's family, friends, fun and football! Wouldn't it be great if we could all just tailgate?"

So this fall, when you hitch up your family truckster and prepare your numerous tailgating wares and eats, remember that the modern cultural ritual you are fulfilling on game day finds its humble origins during the tumultuous times following the Civil War. Furthermore, when the unruly throngs of thousands of well-fed screaming football fans inevitably electrify the night air inside arenas across the country with the deafening roar of their bourbon soaked voices, remember that they are unknowingly reliving the glory and pride of their fallen Civil War brethren.

38   Tailgating with Chef Jeff Warner

JEFF WARNER KNOWS A LITTLE about tailgating. Well, at least he knows a little about the food part. Jeff is a Cajun chef with more than a decade of experience in catering fine food. Jeff has cooked on the Delta Queen Riverboat as well as in Manhattan, New York's Hell's Kitchen. Jeff knows what all tailgater's know—that good food has the effect of bringing people together. My brother has granted us permission to print the secret recipes to a couple of his favorite tailgating dishes—Death Valley Crawfish Etouffeé and Sugar Bowl Seafood Jambalaya. We hope you enjoy these tailgating treats as much as our friends and family have through the years. And remember . . . the next time you're in Baton Rouge and you want Chef Jeff Warner to cater your tailgating party, give him a call in advance at:

(225) 248-9903 or(225) 281-3319

Death Valley Crawfish Étouffée

Ingredients

3 lbs. Louisiana crawfish tails	2 bell peppers
1/2 cup of crawfish fat	2 onions
1 cup of chopped parsley	1 bunch of celery
2 cups of green chopped onions	1 cup of flour
3 tablespoons mashed roasted garlic	1 cup of oil
Cajun seasoning to taste	Salt & Hot Sauce
1 tablespoon of paprika	Water as needed

Death Valley Crawfish Étouffée directions

Using flour and oil, make a light golden brown roux. Add all of chopped onion, peppers celery and garlic. Cook until onions are tender. Add crawfish and fat, cook for 20 minutes. Add very little water; slowly add water a little at a time. Your étouffée should begin to thicken up; it should be very thick, start to add paprika and season to taste. Throw in some of those great chopped green onions and serve over some of that fluffy Louisiana rice. Enjoy!

Note: *Shrimp, lump crabmeat, or chicken are also great substitutes. Best when served on cold game days with the smell of a win in the air!*

Sugar Bowl Seafood Jambalaya

Ingredients:

1 lb. shrimp 70/90 count, peeled and deveined

1 lb. Louisiana crawfish tails

1 lb. Louisiana crabmeat

1 lb. smoked sausage (cut in half moon)

4 tablespoons vegetable oil	1 cup green onions
1 cup garlic, chopped	1 cup parsley, chopped
2 cups green pepper, diced	2 cup yellow onions, diced
1 cup celery, diced	1 can Rotel
2-3 bay leaves	2 teaspoons dried thyme
3 cups long grain rice (parboiled)	6 cups water (or seafoodstock 2X)

Sugar Bowl Seafood Jambalaya directions

Prepare seafood: clean shrimp, pick crabmeat, strain crawfish tails, keeping fat. Saute' sausage and oil for 3-4 min. Add parsley, onions, bell pepper, celery, and garlic. Cook until vegetables are tender. Add diced can tomatoes, & seafood (except crabmeat). Cook until shrimp is pink. Add seasoning and rice, stirring constantly. Add stock or water, bring to a boil, turn low cook for 25-30 minutes or until rice is fluffy. Lastly, fold in crabmeat, and check to add seasoning. Garnish with green onions. Enjoy! Yields 15-20 portions. Serve With Deep Fried Pistolettes & Potato Salad, & they will definitely come back for more, Cher!

"Bon Appetit, Tiger fans!" —*Chef Jeff*

Victory!

39 Great LSU Football Quotations

"WHAT YOU FIND IN BATON ROUGE is typical of the football frenzy in the South. No city in the country hath greater love for its football team. So deep is the feeling that workers arrange vacations, night shifts, bowling leagues, weddings and even family pregnancies so that they won't conflict with LSU games."

– John D. McCallum on football at LSU

"It's a magical setting, the excitement, the atmosphere, is unmatched anywhere—and I've been in stadiums from one end of America to the other. They ought to put up a statue to the guy who came up with night football at LSU."

– Mike Bynum, sports author

"There are no office hours for champions."

– Paul Dietzel

"The worst mistake any coach can make is not being himself."
— *Charles McClendon*

"In Baton Rouge, it's not a law to love LSU, but the city fathers could probably get one passed if they needed to."
— *Charles McClendon*

"Everybody at LSU wants another great team like '58. The only trouble is that our schedule is so tough, we could have a great year and never know it."
— *Charles McClendon*

"Outside the Louisiana Purchase in 1803, many Cajuns consider Billy Cannon's run the greatest event in state history."
— *Mississippi Head Coach John Vaught,
regarding Billy Cannon's magical romp*

"The athletic field is very democratic. Each person is judged by personal merit rather than personal wealth or prestige."
— *Paul Dietzel*

"I like to throw the ball. To me, the pro game is throwing. I may be wrong, but putting the ball in the air is the way to win."
— *Y.A. Tittle*

"I don't fool around with losers! LSU can't have a losing football team, because that will mean that I am associated with a loser!"
— *Louisiana Governor Huey Pierce Long*

". . . My God, my God, I have so much left to do. Who will look after my darling LSU?"
— *Huey Long's reported last words*

"Encircling itself, high and in the air like a fortress abandoned during some particularly bloodied age, towers the most ferocious address in Louisiana. In Tiger Stadium, a game is not merely seen. It is HEARD. The sound of it twists up the steel and concrete enclosure like a particularly sinister tornado. The parts are played out equally in the stands and on the field. Writers in the press box, high over the crowd, find themselves unable to think when the noise stops. If it stops."

– John Logue

"I'd like to be there when the BCS tries to sort this one out."

– Josh Reed, LSU Biletnikoff Award
winner, after ruining UT's Rose Bowl
chances by defeating the heavily-favored
Vols in the SEC Championship Game in
Atlanta, 2001

"If you're looking back, you're in trouble."
— *"Cholly Mac"*

"There is no single "best" way to do something in football."
— *Charles McClendon*

"I have been blessed to have been associated with some out-standing people and been fortunate to coach and a be a part of so many young men's lives."
— *LSU coach Pete Jenkins, on his retirement from coaching in February, 2002*

"I think a kicker's job is to make sure his name is not mentioned. If it is in the paper, it usually is not a good thing."
— *LSU kicker John Corbello*

"What looked exciting from the stands was really just mud, blood and sweat."
— *Tommy Casanova, three-time All-American*

"Be as positive as you can to everyone you meet and they'll always think you're a winner."

— *Charles McClendon*

"No scholar of the Dixie gridiron can pass his years in this mortal coil without witnessing a night game in Tiger Stadium in Baton Rouge. The sinking burnt-orange Louisiana sun casts death-like shadows upon this terrain of old tumult, and minutes before kickoff the ceaseless mounting clamor rises in synesthesia, making one feel he is in the presence of some elemental phenomenon of near geological propensity."

— *Willie Morris,* The Sporting News

"In football, and in life, you've got to keep proving yourself."

— *Charlie McClendon*

"It's a sad thought in knowing I won't ever run through those goal posts anymore. I can still picture the first time I ran out in Tiger Stadium. It was kind of eerie. I looked around a couple of times – Boy! What a thrill that was! That was some thrill!"
– Pete Jenkins, LSU assistant coach,
upon his retirement in the spring of 2002

"When I became athletic director at LSU the first thing I did was increase the travel budgets for all sports so that when we stay in Starkville we can have rooms without views."
– Skip Bertman

"Starkville is an Indian word for trailer park."
– Skip Bertman

"While focusing on an upcoming opponent, we learned that preparation is important, and that it pays off; that practice and repetition make difficult things second nature; that discipline and self-sacrifice are essential components when working as a team; that eleven players of average ability working together can accomplish more than eleven "stars" playing without a common cause; that people do not demand that you always win but that you always give your best; that you never stop to look at the size of the mountain, you just start climbing, then scratch and climb as hard as you can until time runs out and more often than not you get to the top."

> — *Tommy Casanova, excerpted from the foreword of* A Tailgater's Guide To SEC Football, *by Chris Warner*

"I want my family, players and friends to only share tears of happiness today. Let's all remember the good times while we were together. I have prayed that what little I could contribute to our society would help make the place we live a little better. I challenge my family, players and friends who I love so much to do the same thing. You can do it. Love your family and neighbors as I have loved mine. Commit yourself to do something good for others. My last coaching point: teach the world that the word 'responsibility' means 'your actions.'"

– Charles McClendon, terminally ill with
cancer, Tiger Stadium Memorial service,
Florida game, 2001

40

Distance Chart
From Baton Rouge

(Based on a driving speed of 70 miles per hour)

Atlanta, Georgia . . . . 7 hours
Biloxi, Mississippi . . . . 2 hours
Birmingham, Alabama . . . . . . 6 hours
Dallas, Texas . . . . 6.5 hours
Houston, Texas . . . . 4 hours
Jackson, Mississippi . . . . 2.5 hours
Jacksonville, Florida . . . . 8.5 hours
Little Rock, Arkansas . . . . 5 hours
Mobile, Alabama . . . . 3 hours
Monroe, Louisiana . . . . 2.5 hours
New Orleans, Louisiana . . . . . 1 hour
Orlando, Florida . . . . 10 hours
Pensacola, Florida . . . . 4 hours

41   Fan Websites

TODAY THERE ARE SEVERAL truly great Internet websites with free, updated-daily content available. In addition to lsusports.net, the official website of LSU Athletics, try:

1. **www.dandydon.com**

   This is an LSU fan favorite. Dandy is a former LHSAA football official. Don's network of recruiting contacts keep him firmly " . . . in the loop."

2. **www.tigerdroppings.com**

   One of the better blogger sites with constant "poop" on LSU. If you like to "blog" (engage in weblogs), this is your thing.

3. **www.secsports.com**

   The official website of the Southeastern Conference. Bookmark it for daily updates.

42   Acknowledgments.

To Coach Larry Bielat of Michigan State University, for the inspiration and motivation.

To the LSU Sports Information Department Staff, especially Jason Fierman. Thanks for fulfilling my requests. Your continued efforts to improve LSU's world standing has paid great dividends. Today, LSU's brand as a big-time public institution of higher learning and as a proud athletic member of the Southeastern Conference, is unmistakable.

"The drama of sport is a big part of the drama of life and the scope of this drama is endless."

– Grantland Rice

If you enjoyed this book, you may enjoy others by Chris Warner:

A Tailgater's Guide To SEC Football

SEC Basketball History & Tradition

SEC Baseball History & Tradition

SEC Sports Quotes

SEC Sports Quotes II

The Tiger Among Us,
a novel on international terrorism set at LSU in 1990

Email Chris: cewarner@mindspring.com